To John & [...]

TO one ASS-er

From one

to another

Jim [signature]

MW00876555

Potsdam Mission

Memoir of a U.S. Army Intelligence Officer in Communist East Germany

by

James R. Holbrook

AuthorHouse™
1663 Liberty Drive, Suite 200
Bloomington, IN 47403
www.authorhouse.com
Phone: 1-800-839-8640

First published by AuthorHouse   1/14/2013

ISBN: 978-1-4343-5743-4 (sc)

Printed in the United States of America
Bloomington, Indiana

This book is printed on acid-free paper.

DEDICATION

This book is dedicated to all the men and women who served at the U.S. Military Liaison Mission to the Commander in Chief, Group Soviet Forces, Germany from 1947-1990. Their professionalism, diligence and sacrifices, combined with those of the other Allied Military Liaison Missions' members, played a crucial role in preventing an outbreak of hostilities between NATO and the Warsaw Pact during the Cold War.

ACKNOWLEDGMENTS

A *bol'shoe spasibo* to the following individuals who read and commented on selected chapters or complete, draft versions of this memoir: Rolland Amos, Jeff Barrie, William Burhans, Lester Grau, Bonnie Geppert, David Geppert, Ralph Germaine, Lonnie Knickmeier, Bernie McDaniel, Roger Parloff, Alys Romer, Peter Thorsen, and Nick Troyan. Mary McDaniel deserves a special note of appreciation for applying her professional editing expertise to an early version of my manuscript. I continued to make revisions after receiving all their valuable comments, so any mistakes in the final book are mine.

My research on the British Military Liaison Mission was greatly facilitated by Katherine Morris and Betty Morris who went to great efforts to acquire for me hard-to-find books in Great Britain.

I am obliged to the "founding fathers" of the USMLM Association, Tom Spencer and Angel Gonzalez for creating a focal point for USMLM veterans to gather and share experiences and information. Angel also set up the association website from which I was able to glean much useful information for this book. Thanks also to president William Burhans who has done so much to keep the Association active.

CONTENTS

Part IV: Interpreting and Departure

LIST OF PHOTOS

Most photos in this book are from the author's personal files, including the official U.S. Army photos that were given to him at the time of the various events. Ed Hamilton contributed the photo of his car that was rammed by the East Germans. Ralph Germaine graciously provided the remainder. Dion Good prepared the maps.

Photo 1: The Potsdam House with one of USMLM's Opels parked in front.

Photo 2: USMLM Operations Building in Berlin.

Photo 3: License plate on front and rear of all USMLM vehicles.

Photo 4: USMLM vehicle rammed by East Germans in 1997.

Photo 5: The author and Al Jarreau at Wisconsin Boys' State, 1957.

Photo 6: Seaman Recruit Holbrook, U.S. Naval Reserve, 1957.

Photo 7: The author in dress uniform at Annapolis, 1959.

Photo 8: Private First Class Holbrook, 1961.

Photo 9: Top page of author's first Russian test at Monterey.

Photo 10: Teufelsberg, Berlin.

Photo 11: The author as a staff sergeant and graduate student at The American University, 1966.

Photo 12: The author with Army helicopters, 1967.

Preface to Second Edition

The declassification in 2006 of the 1968 Unit History for the United States Military Liaison Mission presented me the opportunity to further elaborate on the early warning service —Imminence of Hostilities—that Allied Missions performed. 1968 was the year of the Warsaw Pact invasion of Czechoslovakia. Imminence of Hostilities is now covered in a new Chapter 12.

At a 2007 reunion in the Washington, DC area, I was able to talk with former Mission colleagues who provided me with valuable comments and recommendations. It was there I renewed my acquaintance with Sergeant Jim Rice, one of my drivers in 1976-77. Consequently, I am now able to include Sergeant Rice by name in the events described in Chapter 14. Ed Hamilton and Mike Crutcher questioned my reference to the Soviet T-72 tank in the first edition of *Potsdam Mission*. Although the 1976 Unit History does use that nomenclature for the tank that was introduced during my service at the Mission, it appears we were confused at the time. The tank turned out to be the T-64, a point that was apparently cleared up by the end of 1977.

Finally, I am now able to include some examples from a partial dossier kept on me by the East German secret police (MfS). Unfortunately, it is far from complete.

James R. Holbrook
October 2007
potsdammission@yahoo.com

Author's Note

From shortly after the end of World War II to the end of the Cold War, American, British and French Military Liaison Missions traveled throughout Communist East Germany, collecting and reporting intelligence on the Soviet and East German armies. Soviet military personnel did the same in West Germany. Our status derived from agreements at the end of the war that set up military liaison missions to each other's headquarters. Initially focused on liaison, our activities quickly evolved into intelligence collection operations that led to many dangerous encounters with the Soviet and East German armies. Shootings and vehicle rammings occurred frequently. On occasion, our officers and noncommissioned officers were seriously injured. Before it all ended with the collapse of the Iron Curtain, one French sergeant and one American officer had been killed.

I served in this unique military unit in 1976-77. This memoir dramatizes my impressions, responses to, and interpretations of events and experiences during that phase of my military career. My duty with the United States Military Liaison Mission (USMLM), together with the years I spent preparing for such an assignment, played an important role in shaping my evolving views on military intelligence, the Soviet Army, Russians and the Soviet Union. Although I draw upon recently declassified historical documents to add depth and context to my own experiences, this book makes no pretense to being a history of USMLM.

I kept no diary or notes on my experiences during my years in intelligence. I could not, because the notes would have been classified and I had no place to legally store such materials as I moved around to other Army assignments and, finally, retired. Therefore, this memoir is based primarily on my firsthand recollections and impressions. It contains, however, information previously unknown to the public.

The dramatized accounts in this book of my experiences are not precise transcripts of what actually happened, but the essence of those events, as I remember them. That applies particularly to the dialogue I have written to accompany my stories. That said, I find it remarkable I'm still able to recall some dialogue portrayed in the book almost word-for-word as it occurred.

When I arrived to serve at USMLM in the summer of 1976, I brought with me fifteen years as a Russian linguist and analyst of Soviet political and military affairs. That knowledge was important in coloring my early views of both the Soviet Army and military intelligence. Consequently, in chapters 3-9, I've highlighted the key events that led to my becoming a Russian language and Soviet specialist.

Many events in that period of my Army service are still vivid. Others are somewhat vague. I can't remember the names of all the individuals with whom I shared some of these experiences. Even the names of some of the people who helped me greatly in my career continue to elude me. For example, I no longer remember the name of the first-sergeant of the Student Company at the National Security Agency in 1964-65. It was he who pointed out to me an opportunity to finish my undergraduate work at a civilian university while still an enlisted man on active duty. This turned out to be a seminal event for my future.

Since I couldn't locate some individuals who accompanied me on several of the intelligence missions described in this book, I've omitted some names. In doing this, I may have done a disservice to two people in particular: then Staff Sergeant Karl Mabardy and Sergeant Hans Tiffany. They, in addition to Staff Sergeant Ralph Germaine and Sergeant Jim Rice (whom I do include by name in the memoir), were the noncommissioned officers-drivers with whom I did all my "touring" in East Germany. All were expert drivers as well as brave and reliable colleagues during our missions in East Germany. I'm very proud to have served with them.

The catalyst for writing this memoir was the recent declassification of several USMLM unit histories, which I obtained via the USMLM Association website. These histories have permitted me to broach subjects that were previously unavailable to the general public. The classified activities revealed in these histories add an important dimension to the experiences of all former Mission personnel who "toured" throughout East Germany. The Mission's contribution to U.S. intelligence during the Cold War cannot be fully appreciated without knowledge of its classified work. Those histories jogged my memory and provided some specific details of events I had long forgotten. I have also used some other accounts of intelligence activities in Berlin that provide background for the *raison d'être* of USMLM and certain of its operations.

Although the USMLM unit histories were an invaluable source for me, as they can be for others attempting to recreate their past experiences, they do not tell the whole story. Any comprehensive history of USMLM must include "the stories behind the stories." Authors of the USMLM official histories for 1964-67 attempted to do just that—to include some details behind several events. The histories for those years include a section entitled "The Story Behind the Report." Unfortunately, that section in USMLM histories was later discontinued. The reader will see, from my occasional insertion of the official historical record into this book, how the personal story behind an incident adds important, interesting details and, in some cases, even contradicts the official version.

Hundreds of personal stories—many more dramatic than mine, some truly heroic—by "Missionaries" with much longer service than mine at USMLM (some officers and NCOs served at the Mission three different times) can reveal more completely the human side of what transpired during the Mission's history. They would be stories of men who risked their personal safety while operating in the midst of some 350,000 Soviet and 105,000 East German military personnel, plus the East German police and East German security service personnel.

The public deserves a comprehensive history of USMLM much like the ones written about the British Military Liaison Mission. Such a history can be written, however, only if a historian is willing to supplement the official unit histories with interviews of as many former members of this unique unit as possible. A complete history of USMLM is a task of some urgency, since USMLM no longer exists, and those who served in Potsdam and Berlin during several critical periods in U.S. history will not be with us much longer.

I call upon other "Missionaries," especially former U.S. Air Force Team members, to write about their experiences before it is too late.

James R. Holbrook
Hacienda de los Piñones
Walsenburg, Colorado
October 2007

ABBREVIATIONS, ACRONYMS AND JARGON

Akt	Soviet term for a protocol, or report, of an incident
APC	Armored personnel carrier
ASA	Army Security Agency
BRIXMIS	British Military Liaison Mission
CENTAG	Central Army Group
CI	Counterintelligence
CINC	Commander in Chief
Clobbered	Detained by the Soviets or East Germans
CRITIC	The highest U.S. message priority
DAO	Defense Attaché Office
Deadman	Steel plate secured to ground with a stake, in the absence of a tree nearby, for attaching a winch.
FAO	Foreign Area Officer
FMLM	1. French Military Liaison Mission (in French—MMFL) 2. Translation of the Soviet abbreviation for all foreign military liaison missions
FSB	Fire Support Base
GDR	German Democratic Republic (East Germany)

GRU	Glavnoye razvedevatel'noe upravlenie (Soviet Military Intelligence)
GSFG	Group of Soviet Forces, Germany
Hootch	Living quarters (term used by U.S. personnel in Vietnam)
ICD	Imitative Communications Deception
IIFFV	Second Field Force, Vietnam
IIR	Intelligence Information Report
IOH	Imminence of Hostilities
MfS	Ministerium für Staatssicherheit (East German secret police)
MI	Military Intelligence
MR	Motorized Rifle (the Soviet name for units that are similar to a U.S. mechanized infantry unit)
MRD	Motorized Rifle Division
MRR	Motorized Rifle Regiment
MRS	Mission Restriction Sign
MVD	Ministerstvo vnutrennikh del (Ministry of Internal Affairs. One of the precursors to the KGB. Today the MVD are the civil police in Russia.)
Nark	Mission jargon for any surveillant
NCO	Noncommissioned officer
NKVD	Narodnyj komissariat vnutrennikh del, a pre-KGB

	designation of the Soviet secret police
NVA	1. National Volksarmee (East German Armed Forces)
	2. North Vietnamese Army
OSS	Office of Strategic Services
Plebe	A first-year midshipman at Annapolis, or cadet at West Point
PRA	Permanent Restricted Area
RDF	Radio direction finding
SERB	Soviet External Relations Bureau (Our direct contact for logistic support and business with HQ GSFG)
SIGINT	Signals Intelligence, acquired by monitoring electronic transmissions
SIS	Secret Intelligence Service (British)
SMLM-F	Soviet Military Liaison Mission, Frankfurt (in American Zone)
SOU	Special Operations Unit
SOXMIS	Soviet Military Liaison Mission, Bünde (British Zone)
Sovs	Short for "Soviets"
Stasi	Nickname for agents of the East German secret police, MfS
Top	Highest ranking sergeant in a unit, usually a first-sergeant
TRA	Temporary Restricted Area

UAZ	Soviet jeep-like vehicle (pronounced 'OO-ahs')
UG and KS	Ustav garnizonnoj i karaulnoj sluzhby (Manual of Garrison and Guard Duties)
USAREUR	U.S. Army, Europe
USARI	U.S. Army Russian Institute in Garmisch, Germany
USMLM	U.S. Military Liaison Mission
VOPO	Volkspolizei (East German police)
VRN	Vehicle registration number

PART I: IN THE MIDDLE OF 350,000 SOVIET TROOPS

CHAPTER 1
MY FIRST "CLOBBER"

1976. A slight but bitter wind drifted in from the Mecklenburger Bucht, just off the Baltic Sea. At six o'clock in the morning the light was already beginning to appear. It was only the middle of September, so the cold snap that had descended on us the day before caught us unprepared. The damp air cut through our light uniforms.

We had been traveling and collecting intelligence in northern East Germany for two days, but now our mission was complete. There had been no complications. We were headed home, a full day's drive to Potsdam and Berlin. Our Ford Bronco's special, 35-gallon gas tank was nearing one-quarter full, so we stopped at an "Intertank" gas station along Route 105, the Wismar-Rostock highway. My driver, Staff Sergeant Ralph Germaine, having prepaid for the gas, stood outside in the cold, filling the tank. I remained inside the warm car. In my mind, I was already formulating an outline for the intelligence reports I would file upon return to Berlin.

Sergeant Germaine tapped on the window and motioned to our rear. I cracked the window. "Sir, we got company," he said.

I turned to see that a Soviet jeep-like vehicle, an UAZ-469, had pulled into the parking area and stopped. A Soviet lieutenant got out of the jeep and started walking toward us.

"Get back in the car," I instructed Sergeant Germaine who hurriedly replaced the fuel hose and jumped into the car.

"Lock the doors, Ralph," I said.   I got out of the Bronco and walked to meet the officer, hoping to stop him before he reached our vehicle.   Although blankets covered our intelligence gear and curtains masked the back windows, I didn't want the Soviet lieutenant looking through the side windows.   He might pose questions about the unusual buttons and toggle switches on our dashboard.

"Let me see your documents," he said in Russian.

"Good morning to you too, Lieutenant," I replied in Russian.   "What's this all about?"

"You're in a restricted area."

"No we're not."

"You may not realize it, but you are in a *PZR*."   The lieutenant used the Soviet abbreviation for what we called a Permanent Restricted Area (PRA).

"Nonsense," I replied, "I'll show you.   Wait here a minute."   I returned to the car, signaled for Sergeant Germaine to unlock my door, reached in and pulled out a map.

"Here, take a look for yourself," I said when I returned.   "This is the PRA map issued by your own headquarters."

He casually glanced at the map, then looked up at me again.   "Your documents."

I handed him my Soviet pass—the document the Soviet Army headquarters provided Allied Mission officers and their drivers. These passes authorized us to travel throughout East Germany. He looked it over, then eyed me up and down.

"Get back in your vehicle and follow me to the *komendatura*," he ordered. "I'll return your pass when this is sorted out." Every East German city where Soviet troops were stationed had a *komendatura* that was roughly equivalent to a U.S. provost marshal's office or a military police station. In some ways, the *komendants* were local military governors in the Soviet Occupational Zone.

I got back into the Bronco.

"What's up, sir? What do we do?" Sergeant Germaine looked over at me. In fact, his eyes were asking me, "Do we make a run for it?"

I quickly answered his nonverbal question. "No, hold it. He kept my pass. We're going to have to follow him to the *komendatura*."

"Roger that, sir."

The UAZ pulled out and we fell in behind. The Soviet driver drove slowly through the deserted streets of Wismar. The lieutenant had turned in his seat and was watching us through his back window the entire way to the *komendatura*.

Sergeant Germaine smiled. "Your first clobber, sir?"

"Yeah. Well, I guess it had to happen sooner or later."

"Clobber" was the term we used to denote an arrest or detention by the Soviets or East Germans. This was my first clobber in the two months since I had arrived at the Mission and had begun going on intelligence collection trips. Clobbers occurred from time to time with tour officers of all the Allied Missions—usually without any serious consequences. But I had read reports of some detentions that turned out very unpleasantly. Most of those, however, had occurred when Soviet soldiers in the field, often near a Soviet training area, detained a Mission team.

So I had been detained in Wismar, East Germany, by a Soviet lieutenant who was taking me to the local military police station. I mused to myself, "So, here's little Jimmy Holbrook from DeSoto, Wisconsin. Now 36 years old and a major in the U.S. Army. In hot water." After 15 years of studying and analyzing the Soviet Army from afar—and safely from behind a desk—I was about to have my first face-to-face hostile encounter with Soviet Army officers.

My casual response to Sergeant Germaine's question about this being my first clobber masked the fear that was starting to overtake me. The adrenalin flare-up from my brief argument with the Soviet lieutenant lingered. What would happen next? I knew that shortly I would be separated from my driver and vehicle and would be entirely in Soviet hands. That alone frightened me. During clobbers, the officer would go into a *komendatura*, while the driver stayed in the vehicle and kept it secure from outsiders. Memories of nightmares I had over the last ten years or so about being helpless during Soviet KGB interrogations, absurd though they might have been, flashed before me.

I hadn't been in a PRA. I wasn't taking pictures of military facilities. I was authorized by the Soviets to travel in East Germany. Nonetheless, my study of Soviet history and their intelligence services' brutal handling of prisoners made it quite clear that nothing could protect me if the Soviets decided to violate my rights. Would there be Soviet intelligence officers at the *komendatura*? Had they been waiting for me and sent this military policeman, if that's what he really was? I was sure we had avoided surveillance by the Soviets and East Germans during the last few hours. Maybe, I tried to assure myself, I would be lucky this time and would be dealing only with regular Soviet army officers and not their intelligence types.

When we arrived at the *komendatura*, the lieutenant motioned for me to follow him. I had already handed my exposed film and incriminating notes to Sergeant Germaine. I grabbed the PRA map, got out of the Bronco and followed him into the building. As the door closed behind me, I felt my body tense. Now I was really isolated. I didn't even have the relative security of our Mission vehicle, which was supposed to enjoy diplomatic extraterritoriality. All I had on my side was my status as an accredited liaison officer to the Commander in Chief (CINC) of the Soviet Army in Germany.

"Come in here and have a seat. I'll be right back," the lieutenant said as he flipped a light switch. He motioned to the only chair in the room and then left, closing the door behind him. A single light bulb hanging from the ceiling cast anemic light throughout the room. I looked around. The room looked like a Hollywood-designed KGB interrogation chamber, minus torturing devices. It was stark, containing only the chair and one small desk with nothing on it. A rolled-up map hung on the wall next to pictures of Lenin and Brezhnev. I was so cold I decided not to sit down. Instead, I paced the floor to keep warm. I wasn't sure whether the shivering was from the cold or from my being nervous. Probably from both. I stopped once to look out the small window in the room, hoping to see something of interest. I saw only a motor park with a few trucks and jeeps in it.

In a couple minutes, I heard the lieutenant on the phone. His loud voice was penetrating the wall and I could hear bits of his side of the conversation.

"American soldiers... Restricted area... Here at the *komendatura*..."

Since I knew he was engaged, I walked over to the map on the wall and pulled on the string. Perhaps, I thought, there would be some good Order of Battle (OB) intelligence here. To my disappointment, however, it was only a normal map of East and West Germany. A thick black line depicted the Intra-German border, but the map was completely devoid of any symbols or handwriting.

The lieutenant stopped talking. I rolled the map back up and stepped away. He didn't return immediately to the room. With whom had he been talking on the phone? Why hadn't he or anyone else come back into the room? How long was I going to be here alone? How much did the Soviets know about my background? If they had a dossier on me, would they have a file out here in the boonies?

I continued to walk around the room, trying to keep my imagination in check. The old nightmares once again became vivid. It seems silly now and perhaps was irrational even then. But at the time, I couldn't get the dreams out of my mind. Those nightmares began to mix eerily with memories of my Plebe year at Annapolis. For example, at the Naval Academy, upperclassmen used a hazing technique we called the "green bench." They would say, "hit the green bench, mister," and we would have to place our backs against a wall, then slide down the wall until we were in a sitting position. We were required to remain in that position until the upper classman allowed us to stand up, or we fell down. That reminded me of a form of torture Robert Conquest reported in his book *The Great Terror.* The Soviet NKVD (one of the precursors to the KGB) called it the *stoika*. The technique was to make a prisoner stand on his tiptoes for hours.

Of course my nightmares were much more violent than any Plebe-year hazing. In the dreams I was often arrested or kidnapped and tortured by the KGB. The most graphic torture I remembered was being stripped naked and thrown against the wall of my cold cell. Those nightmares, and the knowledge that someday I would likely come into contact with Soviet intelligence, suggested to me that I should try to prepare myself for torture. But how does one prepare? One never knows how he or she will react until the event actually occurs. Besides, there was no history of Allied Mission personnel ever being tortured. Roughed up from time to time, but never really tortured. Then again, not all the Mission officers were intelligence officers. Did the Soviets know of my past intelligence assignments at the signals intelligence site in Berlin in 1963-64 or, later, at the National Security Agency?

In what seemed to be hours, but was probably only about 15 minutes, the door opened and a major walked in, followed by the lieutenant. Seeing that I was standing, the major took the chair and placed it behind the desk and sat down. He was wearing a rumpled everyday uniform and had not put on a tie. His eyes were swollen and his nose was red. He reeked of vodka and garlic. It was obvious to me that he had been summoned from his bed or was still partying somewhere when he received the news that two Americans had been "captured." That was good. It meant he was probably not a professional intelligence officer who had been standing by, waiting for me to be brought in.

"The lieutenant says you speak Russian," he said to me. "So, tell me. What's this all about?"

"We were minding our own business, refueling our vehicle. In an open area, at least a mile from any restricted area. The lieutenant here stopped and accused us of violating a PRA."

"Were you in a PRA?"

"No. I just told you that. Not even close."

The major took out an olive-drab handkerchief and wiped his eyes. He then looked at me for a few moments. "How is it you speak Russian the way you do? Are you of Russian extraction?"

"No, but I've studied the language for several years."

The major continued to stare at me for a few seconds, then turned to the lieutenant. "He says he wasn't in a restricted area."

The lieutenant said nothing. I pulled the PRA map out of my pocket and handed it to the major. He looked at it for some time, apparently not knowing exactly how to read it. I walked over and stood beside him.

"Permit me, major," I said and put my finger on Wismar. Then I pointed to the edge of the PRA. "We were here when we were detained. The PRA starts here."

The major studied the map for a few minutes. He seemed intrigued, as if he had never seen such a map. His eyes wandered all over the sheet, then returned to where I indicated our location.

"You woke me up for this?" the major glared at the lieutenant.

I breathed a quiet sigh of relief. The major appeared to have no special interest in me.

"Yes, Comrade Major. According to our information the gas station is in a PRA."

"Wait a minute," I said. I took the map from the major and walked over to the lieutenant. I pointed to the writing at the top of the map "PERMANENT RESTRICTED AREAS, SOVIET OCCUPIED ZONE."

"Your own HQ gave us this map. Look here. See how far the PRA border is from the gas station?"

The lieutenant remained silent. The major got up and left the room, followed by the lieutenant. Soon I heard the major on the phone. He spoke louder than the lieutenant had earlier. It seemed to me all Soviets talked loud when they were on the telephone, but perhaps the longer the distance of the call, the louder they felt they must shout. I could hear almost everything the major said. He was talking to the Soviet External Relations Bureau (SERB) in Potsdam, the office through which the Mission conducted its affairs with Soviet Headquarters.

"My goddammed lieutenant pulled in an American team and brought them to the *komendatura*. From what I can determine, they weren't doing anything wrong and were not in a restricted area. I've seen their map."

Silence, as the major listened to the speaker on the other end.

"But what am I supposed to do with them?"

More silence.

"*Yest, tovarisch podpolkovnik.* (Yes sir, Comrade Lieutenant Colonel. Will do.)"

At that the telephone conversation apparently ended. But the major didn't stop shouting.

"You dumb son-of-a-bitch. You've caused all kinds of trouble here. Now we have to file a bunch of reports. The Americans may lodge a protest."

"But, Comrade Major..."

"Shut up. You've done enough tonight. Give the American back his pass and release him."

The major never returned to my room. The lieutenant came in with a sheepish grin on his face and handed me my pass.

"You may go now," he said quietly. "But you are to stay out of restricted areas."

"Sure. I'll keep that in mind." I said as I took the pass and rejoined Sergeant Germaine in the Bronco.

As we headed for Potsdam and Berlin, I began to evaluate my first clobber. First of all, I considered myself fortunate not to have been interrogated by Soviet security personnel. Of course the major would file a report, but the danger I so exaggerated in my mind was behind me. This time. Second, although my Russian language ability had piqued the major's interest, he didn't question me any more on my background. My Russian had already raised intense curiosity at some of the social functions with the Soviets in Potsdam since my arrival at the Mission. Third, there appeared to have been no special effort to target me personally. After all my years as a Soviet/Russian specialist, this was a big relief. Fourth, the interaction between the lieutenant and the major was as human, and as military, as it might have been in my own army: a zealous young lieutenant and a grizzled, hung-over major.

Finally, I was no longer virgin. I had taken one more step toward becoming a real, touring collection officer. I believed I handled myself well. This first clobber had given me a small dose of confidence. Still, I knew there would be many other incidents and challenges. It was not likely future clobbers would all be as easy as this one.

This clobber would go into the official 1976 USMLM Unit History as:

> 11 September 1976. A short detention of slightly over an hour occurred when a USMLM tour stopped for gas at an Intertank station west of Wismar. A Soviet officer accused the tour of being in a PRA and escorted them to the Wismar Kommandatura. The problem was caused by the Soviet hand-drawn PRA map which was at variance with the USMLM version. A call from the Wismar Kommandant to Potsdam (SERB) validated the USMLM position and permitted continuation of the tour. Once again, the Soviets were correct and proper in their demeanor.

CHAPTER 2
UNITED STATES MILITARY LIAISON MISSION

What kind of an organization was the United States Military Liaison Mission? How did it come to pass that in 1976 American soldiers could be running around Communist East Germany, collecting intelligence information? To answer these questions we need to make a brief excursion into history.

Most Americans are unaware that from 1947 to 1990 an American military unit was attached to the Soviet Army headquarters in East Germany. In fact, until 1974 when the United States extended diplomatic recognition to the German Democratic Republic (GDR), USMLM was the only official American presence in East Germany. Located near Potsdam, just outside Berlin, the USMLM compound was the only place in that Communist country where the American flag flew 24 hours a day.

When I signed in at the Mission on July 30th, 1976, I quickly realized I had become a member of an organization specially created to participate in the Allies' occupation of defeated Nazi Germany. Only a few weeks after the 1944 Normandy invasion, the Allies agreed to exchange military liaison missions in connection with their post-war occupation zones in Germany. For me the year 1944 was only a dim memory. In 1944 I was eating graham crackers and taking naps on my little rug at a Hammond, Indiana, kindergarten.

World War II ended in 1945. Almost two years later, on April 5th, 1947, U.S. Lieutenant General Huebner and Soviet Colonel General Malinin signed an agreement that established the U.S. and Soviet Military Liaison Missions. (See Appendix A). Great Britain had already reached a similar agreement with the Soviets in September 1946; the French did the same on April 3rd, 1947.

There are a couple of possible explanations why it took nearly two years to establish the military liaison missions. First, there may have been no urgent need for the missions immediately following the war. Communication between the respective headquarters was already established and may have been still relatively smooth and effective, helped by the goodwill created during the combined Allied efforts to defeat Germany. That didn't last long, however, and soon all sides adopted more suspicious attitudes. By the end of 1946, all four Allied occupying armies saw the need to have liaison teams in each others' occupation zones, if for no other reason than to monitor compliance with agreements on the administration of defeated Germany.

It may also be that the U.S. Forces for intelligence information linked the timing of the Huebner-Malinin Agreement to a critical need. David Murphy, Sergei Kondrashev, and George Bailey's book *Battleground Berlin* informs us that until 1947, U.S. and British intelligence used German agents in the Soviet Zone who provided excellent information on airfields, barracks, troop movements, ammunition dumps, training areas, fortifications and troop maneuvers. In 1946, however, the Soviets began arresting these agents, and in March 1947 they "rolled up the entire net." The next month USMLM was established. U.S. and British intelligence would now have to rely on their military missions for day-to-day monitoring of Soviet occupation forces.

Curiously, the U.S./Soviet Huebner-Malinin Agreement differed significantly from the agreements between the Soviets and the other Allies. In the case of USMLM, it provided for 14 military personnel, with no restrictions on rank. The British/Soviet Robertson-Malinin Agreement, on the other hand, allowed for 31 military personnel (11 officers and 20 enlisted), while the French/Soviet Noiret-Malinine Agreement allowed for 18 personnel (6 officers and 12 enlisted). Thus, the British Mission (BRIXMIS) had almost the same number of military representatives as the French (FMLM) and American Missions combined. The Americans had the smallest number of all.

The difference in numbers of personnel for each country's missions may have been the result of quickly deteriorating relations among the World War II Allies between September 1946, when the British signed their agreement with the Soviets, and April 1947, when the French and Americans signed. By the spring of 1947, it is also possible both the Soviet and the American sides feared having too many troops who had now become Cold War opponents in their respective zones. Certainly the relative importance of the U.S., British and French contributions to the Soviet victory in World War II might suggest the United States should have been the largest of the three Missions. Despite the Soviet Union's heroic and critical contribution to the defeat of Hitler's forces overall, it is doubtful their victory on the Eastern Front would have been possible without American Lend-Lease. But that kind of logic didn't rule the day in 1947.

I often refer in this book to Potsdam and Berlin. Where exactly was USMLM located? We had two bases of operations: a residence estate in Potsdam, East Germany, and a secure facility in West Berlin.

Our estate in East Germany, like the Soviets' facility in Frankfurt, West Germany, was supposed to enjoy, according to the Huebner-Malinin Agreement, "full rights of extraterritoriality." On a couple of occasions, as you will read later, this provision was ignored by the East Germans.

In East Germany, the Soviet Army turned over to USMLM the estate of Prince Sigismund of Prussia. It was located at Am Lehnitzsee 2 in Neu Fahrland, a suburb of Potsdam. The estate was a 3-acre lakefront property, built early in the 20th century by a Prussian Army officer. It contained a 3-story mansion, two 2-story houses, and combination garage-stable-living quarters. In 1976, when I was at the Mission, only the main house was habitable.

Prince Sigismund of Prussia, a member of the royal Hohenzollern family bought the estate in 1925. His father was a brother of Kaiser Wilhelm II. Shortly thereafter, the prince was killed in a riding accident, but his widow and son, Prince Friedrich Karl, remained in the house until the last days of World War II, departing just as the Soviet Army approached. To this day the Germans know the estate informally as "Villa Sigismund." We called it the "Potsdam House." For a short time after the war, the Soviets billeted troops in the mansion and other buildings on the estate. While there, the Soviets used the grounds to raise pigs. After the reunification of Germany in 1990, and the departure of USMLM, the Potsdam House was used by various private organizations until recently, when it was finally returned to the Hohenzollern family.

Photo 1: The Potsdam House with one of USMLM's Opels parked in front.

In 1976, an officer-in-charge (OIC) of the Potsdam House lived there on a permanent basis. During my assignment with USMLM, the OIC was First-Lieutenant Howard Berner, a former Russian student of mine at West Point. Howie supervised nine East German staff: four cooks/waitresses, three cleaning women, one gardener, and one mechanic. He also dealt with the Soviets on matters of logistic support. The Soviets provided coal, rations, trash pickup, utilities, gasoline and telephone service. The

U.S. military command in West Berlin augmented Soviet support by providing American furniture, additional provisions, and recreational equipment for Mission members and their families when they visited or stayed at the House. East German guards provided 24-hour "security" of the Potsdam House grounds. Except for the Potsdam House OIC, Mission officers, as well as enlisted and civilian staff, lived with their families in American housing in West Berlin.

As the only U.S. presence in East Germany before 1974, the Mission and its personnel occasionally attracted anti-American "spontaneous" government-sponsored demonstrations at the Potsdam House. In July 1958, during the Suez crisis, East German mobs of several hundred people stormed both the BRIXMIS House and the American Potsdam House. In June 1965, anti-Vietnam War protesters assaulted the Potsdam House. They tore down the American flag and ransacked the inside of the mansion. Some of the "students" removed the flag on top of the Potsdam House, painted "Ami [Americans] go home" on it, and draped it across an overturned Mission sedan. That very night, Mission personnel erected a new flagpole and conducted a flag-raising ceremony under floodlights. The Soviets, who may have been somewhat embarrassed to have lost control of their East German underlings, quickly hired East German workmen to repair the House, repaint all the rooms, replace the damaged telephones, and repair the chandeliers.

By the time I arrived at USMLM in 1976, the Potsdam House was used primarily as a jumping-off point for trips into the interior of East Germany. It served also as a place for official meetings and social functions with Soviet and

Allied military representatives, for casual entertainment of guests of Mission members, and for the rest and recreation (R&R) of Mission families. When my family and I stayed at the Potsdam House for our week, we lived like royalty, taking our meals in a formal dining room, replete with servants attending to our needs.

All Mission administration, the processing and storage of classified documents, and all classified briefings and discussions took place at our other base of operations in West Berlin. During the first years of USMLM's existence, our West Berlin base was located in two rooms of the Berlin Command's headquarters compound. In 1952, the USMLM base moved to the Old Press Club on Sven Hedin Strasse in West Berlin. In 1957, the headquarters moved again to a historic Berlin house at 19/21 Foehrenweg, where it remained until disestablishment of USMLM in 1990.

The house on Foehrenweg had been planned and built in 1936 by Albert Speer and was used during World War II as a secret headquarters by Field Marshal Wilhelm von Keitel, Chief of Staff of the German Military High Command. The building had three stories and a usable attic. It contained 33 rooms totaling nearly 9,000 square feet. The lower two levels were bomb-proofed by the Nazis with steel-reinforced concrete floors 2-3 feet thick and walls of similar material, about 18 inches thick. The complex also contained an underground escape tunnel. The OSS and CIA used the building briefly before USMLM moved in. Murphy describes our Berlin operations base as "a building on Foehrenweg, a quiet, tree-lined street in the fashionable suburb of Dahlem that had suffered very little bomb damage.... The building looked like the set for a movie adaptation of a Le Carré novel."

Photo 2: USMLM Operations Building in Berlin.

Supposedly, the number of personnel at the Mission was determined by the Huebner-Malinin Agreement, which stated that personnel at both the American and Soviet Missions would not "exceed fourteen (14) officers and enlisted personnel...[to] include all necessary technical personnel, office clerks, personnel with special qualifications..." The actual number, however, although it varied from year to year, was always more than 14. In 1976, USMLM's personnel included an Army section of 45 personnel, an Air Force section of 16 and one U.S. Marine officer—for a total of 62 military personnel. Four civilians rounded out the Mission roster.

How could we get away with exceeding the agreed-upon number of 14? Since our main base of operations was in West Berlin, the Soviets could not officially monitor how many people we had assigned. The official limit of 14 applied only to USMLM members authorized to be in the Soviet Zone at any one time. The situations for MMFL and BRIXMIS were analogous to ours. (At one time, BRIXMIS had nearly 200 assigned personnel, including at least one Canadian officer in their operations section.) Consequently, all the Allied Missions had a distinct advantage over their Soviet counterparts in West Germany, who were far from any Soviet military support base.

The fourteen Soviet passes, authorizing travel in East Germany, were rotated among a small contingent of officers and noncommissioned officers (NCOs) who performed the actual travel and intelligence collection. Additional support personnel who remained at the Berlin headquarters provided indispensable administrative, analytic, film processing and logistic support.

While I'm describing the personnel situation, I should say something about the special makeup of the Army officer contingent at the Mission. For several years, almost all Army officers at the Mission were products of the Army's Foreign Area Officer (FAO) program. This was my secondary specialty (my primary was military intelligence, but being a FAO played an equally important role in assignments throughout my career). Army FAOs were a good mix of officers who were either military intelligence or combat arms and service officers. All had specialized foreign language and regional skills needed for such assignments as security assistance to foreign countries, strategic and operational planning at various Army levels, and military attachés at American embassies. As part of their specialized training, FAOs usually traveled and studied in their target country. Since, for the most part, this was not possible to do in the Soviet Union, Russian FAOs spent two years in a special course at the U.S. Army Russian Institute (USARI) in Garmisch, Germany. Duty at USMLM obviously called for Russian FAOs, so USMLM became a key assignment.

Although not all Army officers at USMLM spoke Russian well, each officer brought various critical skills to the Mission that were not possessed by some of us who spoke Russian fluently. For example, an infantry, armor or artillery officer with limited Russian-speaking ability was likely to be a much better judge of Soviet tank and artillery developments than I.

Some Mission officers, including a few from the Air Force contingent, had spent years as enlisted intelligence specialists with the Army Security Agency or Air Force Security Service. For example, I served with the Army Security Agency for six years before I became an officer. I already spoke Russian and had advanced degrees when I was commissioned, so I didn't attend USARI or undergo any additional training before I was designated a FAO.

At the outset, the primary task of USMLM was liaison with the Soviet Army headquarters and the handling of affairs for U.S. citizens who might need assistance in the Soviet Occupation Zone. These activities continued throughout USMLM's history, based on the first of a two-part mission statement. Liaison is stipulated in this statement from the 1976 Unit History:

> The primary and unclassified mission of USMLM is to carry out responsibilities for liaison between

CINC, U.S. Army Europe (on behalf of CINC, European Command) and CINC, Group Soviet Forces, Germany (GSFG), and to serve as a point of contact for other U.S. departments and agencies with CINC, GSFG, as may be required. These functions are carried out in accordance with the Huebner-Malinin Agreement of 1947.

Normal day-to-day liaison duties at USMLM consisted primarily of meetings with the Soviets concerning logistic support of Potsdam House or the delivery and reception of formal and informal notes and protests to and from our respective headquarters. Most of these meetings were conducted at SERB in Potsdam at the request of the Mission Chief or the Chief of SERB. High-level official liaison also took place at the Potsdam House during official social gatherings. Often a high-ranking U.S. officer would come in from Heidelberg or other military headquarters in West Germany and meet with his counterpart from the Soviet headquarters.

An interesting situation developed in 1974, when the U.S. and GDR officially exchanged embassies and set up formal diplomatic relations. Up to that time, our government had treated East Germany simply as the Soviet Occupied Zone. During those first post-war years, the Mission's status in East Germany was clear. It was a liaison unit assigned to the World War II victors/occupiers in the eastern part of Germany—the Soviet Army. The Mission did not recognize any East German authority, and when confronted with it, always insisted on seeing a Soviet military officer. All our business would then be conducted through the Soviets. Starting in 1974, however, the United States began to behave in a schizophrenic way.

Even though diplomatic relations between the U.S. and the GDR had become normalized, USMLM continued to operate under the old rules—the Huebner-Malinin Agreement.

Initially, it was an anxious time for USMLM, and many feared the Mission might be closed down. East German authorities might exploit their newly won recognition by the United States to assert some control over USMLM. Fortunately, the Soviets, who still held an iron fist over East German officials, realized that if USMLM were to be disestablished, the Soviet Military Liaison Mission in Frankfurt, West Germany (SMLM-F) would suffer the same fate. To the relief of Washington, European military headquarters, and USMLM officials, the East German government rarely tried to assert its authority in Mission matters. When it did, the Soviets usually stepped in and nipped it in the bud. We suspected that Soviet Military Mission officers were probably running agents in West Germany. Possibly because of this, Soviet Military Liaison Missions there were too valuable to risk any complications with the Western Allies that might threaten the Soviet Missions' continued existence.

Until diplomatic recognition in 1974, USMLM was often called upon to perform functions that U.S. embassies in other foreign countries handled. The Huebner-Malinin Agreement stated "...the missions will have the right to engage in matters of protecting the interests of their nationals... They have a right to render aid to people of their own country..." For USMLM, this included repatriation of defectors, assisting American citizens who may have become lost or injured on the Autobahn from Helmstedt to Berlin, or may have experienced other difficulties in East Germany.

Liaison soon became, however, a secondary task of USMLM. The deterioration of U.S.-Soviet relations after World War II, the loss of the OSS and British Secret Intelligence Service (SIS) agent networks, and the ensuing Cold War soon caused the Mission early in the game to move beyond pure liaison and to conduct intelligence collection operations. In 1976, the second of the two-part mission statement of USMLM read:

> The secondary and CONFIDENTIAL mission is to exploit its liaison status and attendant potential for the collection of intelligence information in East Germany.

Obviously, this was not part of the Huebner-Malinin Agreement. By the time I arrived at the Mission, intelligence collection occupied nearly 90 percent of the USMLM effort. Top priority was given to: 1) information regarding Imminence of Hostilities (IOH), 2) mobile targets that provided equipment details and identification of units, and 3) the activity status in Soviet and East German military installations.

Still, USMLM was not a top-secret military organization. In fact, I never saw a top-secret document there. On the contrary, USMLM personnel lived with their families in West Berlin, wore the distinctive "Potsdam" patch on their uniforms, and openly drove vehicles around the city and in East Germany with strange-looking yellow license plates showing an American flag, a large two-digit number, and lettering on the license plate in the Russian language.

Photo 3: License plate on front and rear of all USMLM vehicles.

Most Mission personnel would be loath to say we were "spies." In the public mind, however, the term "spy" is almost generic for anyone involved in any kind of intelligence collection. From a professional point of view, even intelligence officers at CIA are not, strictly speaking, "spies." When they are operating clandestinely in the field, they are called "case officers." The people who work for them are "agents." The agent collects the information and then passes it to his case officer, who in turn forwards it to analysis and reporting personnel.

Maybe in general terms we were "spies," but few of us would ever claim that designation. It smacks too much of sensationalism. True, we did much of the same type of intelligence collection that agents in East Germany were doing for the OSS and the British SIS before 1947. True, we did sneak around and attempt to mask our specific tasks and we did "spy" on the Soviet and East German forces. But, in contrast to the work of OSS and SIS agents, we did our collection overtly. That is, the Soviets knew our identities and what we were doing. We used vehicles and wore uniforms that clearly marked us as American military. The agents, or "spies" of the OSS and SIS were covert. If the Soviets learned their identity and what they were doing, they would be arrested and tried, or shot. That's exactly what happened to our "spies" in East Germany in 1946-47.

USMLM officers were, in a manner of speaking, agents and reporters all in one. That was not necessarily so with the Soviet Military Liaison Missions operating in West Germany. As I stated earlier, we believed the Soviets acted as case officers, running agents covertly throughout West Germany. An event in the British zone lends some credence to this suspicion. The BRIXMIS Association history of their Mission recounts an incident in Bünde, where the Soviet Military Liaison Mission (SOXMIS) to the British CINC was located. One night a German civilian woke a British officer who lived in a house next to the SOXMIS compound. Thinking he had reached SOXMIS, the German recounted to the astonished British officer his three-week effort recording British troop movements. When he finished, it became his turn to be surprised. The British officer arrested him and sent for the military police.

An intelligence collection mission into East Germany was called a "tour." We referred to each other as "tour officers" and "tour NCOs." (See Appendix E.) Occasionally we called ourselves "missionaries"—a word sometimes used in Soviet documents to refer to members of the Allied Military Liaison Missions. A tour usually consisted of one officer and one NCO who would go out into East Germany with a specific set of intelligence collection tasks. During my time at the Mission, we traveled in Opel sedans or Broncos that were specially modified for our travel and intelligence collection circumstances. A tour normally took 2 to 3 days.

The fact that Mission teams were traveling around East Germany, collecting intelligence information on the Soviet and East German armies, brought them into frequent conflict with their "host," the Soviet Army, or with East German authorities. During USMLM's history, many detentions, shootings, rammings and assaults occurred. For the most part, however, only a few of these incidents reached the press. The most sensational news story occurred toward the end of USMLM's existence in East Germany. In 1985, a Soviet sentry shot a USMLM tour officer, Major Arthur D. Nicholson, Jr. His death was a direct result of the Soviets brutal refusal to administer, or to let his driver administer, first aid.

Before and after this tragedy there were other shooting incidents. In fact, between 1962 and 1990, there were at least 49 shootings, including the 1966 machine-gunning of a USMLM tour vehicle. The passengers, fortunately, escaped unhurt. The other Allied Missions suffered similar assaults. In 1962, a British corporal was seriously injured by gunfire and, like the incident with Major Nicholson, the East Germans who had done the shooting "paid no attention to the British officer's appeals in fluent German to help his driver who was bleeding." In 1973 alone, according to Tony Geraghty's *BRIXMIS*, "The liaison missions' score-card logged a total of nine [shootings], five involving members of USMLM, three aimed at BRIXMIS and one at the French Mission." During the period 1979-85, "British Mission crews had been rammed and detained 25 times, and there had been four shooting incidents. In four instances, BRIXMIS crews had been beaten up or otherwise assaulted." In 1959, an East German Security squad assaulted a U.S. team in their hotel room in Karl-Marx-Stadt (Chemnitz). The East Germans robbed them of all their possessions and broke into their car.

Numerous vehicle rammings over the years injured several Allied Mission personnel. In March 1979, a large Czech-built Tatra-813 truck struck a Mission car, hurtling it off the road. The vehicle turned over twice and landed on its side. The tour officer, Major Ed Hamilton, was injured badly enough that he was incapacitated for six weeks. Soviet personnel broke into the Mission car and removed all the equipment. Ed and I had taught Russian at West Point in the early 1970s and he provided valuable interpreter support for a visit by Soviet General Ivanovsky in 1977 (See Chapter 22). In March 1984, one year before Major Nicholson was shot, a large East German truck rammed a French Mission vehicle, instantly killing French Adjudant-Chef (Sergeant-Major) Mariotti. The premeditated nature of such rammings was confirmed by a statement made once by a Soviet general who told the Chief of USMLM, the next time a certain tour officer went out, "his wife [was] liable to become a widow. He might collide with a tank or a big truck."

Photo 4: Mission vehicle rammed by the East German military in 1979. The passengers, LTC Hamilton and SSG Tiffany, were both seriously injured.

The U.S. military and USMLM officials often tried to downplay incidents with the Soviets or East Germans and resolve them at the Chief of Mission or CINC level. On occasion, however, both Washington and Moscow became involved. These efforts to keep a lid on incidents were important as the years went by because, in many ways, by 1974, USMLM had become a historical anachronism, given the recognition by the United States of both East and West Germany. Publicity, which usually equates to notoriety when it involves intelligence organizations, could have severely hampered the operations of USMLM. Political and diplomatic pressures might even have forced it to be shut down. In fact, in June 1965, the month of the mob riot at the Potsdam House, an East German spokesman called for USMLM to leave the country, as it was "an unnecessary holdover of postwar occupation."

This was the special U.S. military unit in which I served from July 1976 to September 1977. Little did I know, growing up in a small village in Wisconsin in the 1940s-50s, that someday I would find myself dueling with the Soviet Army and the East German security service behind the "Iron Curtain."

Part II: My Road to Potsdam

CHAPTER 3
ANNAPOLIS

In the late 1950s, I was looking forward to becoming an engineer and a naval officer. Within a couple of years of completing high school, however, I realized I was headed in a completely different direction, although I wasn't sure where it would lead. In retrospect it was my experiences at the U.S. Naval Academy that set me on a course of becoming a foreign language specialist. That would lead, during the next fifteen years of my Army career, to assignments that prepared me for USMLM duty. During my last two years of high school, however, all this was the farthest thing from my mind.

In 1958 I graduated from a small high school in rural DeSoto, Wisconsin. Unlike my own children and the current younger generations, I belonged to a cohort that couldn't wait to get out into the world and make its way in life. My classmates came from farms or small towns within a 25-mile radius of my own village of 400 people. Most of us thought nothing was impossible; all we had to do was put our noses to the grindstone and work our way up in whatever field we chose. For a few of us, any career would provide a better life than the one from which we were escaping. Many of my classmates were looking forward to becoming independent farmers. A few were preparing to attend college to become teachers and coaches. Others departed the area right after graduation to take high-paying jobs in the plants and factories of Milwaukee or other cities around the state.

I had what would be considered a successful high school record, getting almost straight As. Since the school was small (I had only 52 classmates in my graduating class), I was able to play varsity sports. Although I was only five-foot-five and weighed only 125 pounds, I played varsity football for four years—every position in the backfield, including fullback. I even played first-string guard on the basketball team. In fact, in the first of several poor judgment calls in my life, I opted for football in high school instead of band when a schedule conflict forced me to make a choice. To this day, I regret not having pursued music. Did I think I was going to be a college or professional football player when I grew up?!

My college-prep program was heavy on mathematics and the sciences. I should have known there was something wrong when, in my junior and senior years, I ran out of courses at DeSoto High School and could take advanced math classes only by correspondence from the University of Wisconsin. Another shortcoming of my high school didn't really register until after I went to college; DeSoto High offered no foreign languages.

By the end of high school, I'd been class president twice and president of the student council. The high school faculty chose me to represent DeSoto at the statewide American Legion's Boys' State. The enthusiasm I gained from being the campaign manager for Al Jarreau and helping him get elected as Governor of Boys' State in 1957 followed me back to DeSoto. There I organized the Vernon County Young Democrats and the Teens Against Polio. When I graduated high school, I believed there were no limits to what I might be able to accomplish.

Photo 5: The author and Al Jarreau at Wisconsin Boys' State, 1957.

In order to succeed at anything significant in life, however, I was convinced I had to go to college. No one in my family had ever done that. My stepfather's $3000-a-year railroad salary barely sustained our family. As I was growing up, we raised our own vegetables, fished, and hunted. Most of the meat we ate was wild game. There was no way I could count on financial support for college from my family.

I competed (unsuccessfully) for a Trane Company scholarship that would have supported me in an engineering program at LaCrosse State College. This was my first setback in life and quite a shock for an ambitious and confident young high school junior. In March 1957, I joined the U.S. Naval Reserve, partly as a way to earn some extra money by attending the weekly meetings and the active-duty training in the summer. The summer before my senior year, I went through boot camp at the Great Lakes Naval Center and took a two-week cruise on a Navy minesweeper on Lake Michigan.

By 1958, influenced by my reserve training and the encouragement of Navy Commander Chuck Dahl of my reserve unit, I began to think about going to the U.S. Naval Academy in Annapolis. My mother discouraged me from applying for that prestigious school because she didn't want me to be disappointed again. No one in my school had ever attended one of the service academies. The last person in all of Vernon County to attend Annapolis was a boy from Hillsboro, who later rose to prominence in the World War II Pacific Theater as Vice-Admiral Marc Mitscher.

Nevertheless, I couldn't be dissuaded. Poring over the recruiting materials the Academy sent me, I could even see myself in a midshipman's uniform, standing in the pictures in one of the brochures. I decided to apply for an appointment through the Naval Reserve and from my Congressman Gardner Withrow, a Republican. There was little chance of my getting the nod from Congressman Withrow, since my picture had appeared in local newspapers participating in Democratic Party functions. But I didn't let that stop me. Several influential men from Boys' State agreed to write letters to the congressman in support of my appointment. I was soon the proud recipient of a principal appointment from the Naval Reserve and a first-alternate from the congressman. If I could pass the written and physical exams, I was in.

In July 1958 I became a midshipman Plebe, a freshman, at Annapolis. Plebe summer was a challenge, both physically and mentally, as upperclassmen bore down on us, trying to weed out the weak ones, or the ones who weren't motivated enough to stay. I marched more during the first year at Annapolis, than I did during my whole career in the Army.

Photo 6: Seaman Recruit Holbrook, U.S. Naval Reserve, 1957.

Photo 7: The author in dress uniform at Annapolis, 1959.

My first real awareness of contemporary world events took place during that Plebe summer. During one session at the firing range, our Marine instructors never showed up after lunch. We learned later that President Eisenhower had sent 10,000 Marines to Lebanon as part of the precautions taken after a military coup in Baghdad promised to set the Mideast aflame.

During my time at the Academy, my classmates and I engaged in many exciting and informative training exercises, especially during the summer training periods. During Third-Class (sophomore) summer, for example, we sailed on destroyers in the North Atlantic, eventually meeting up with and escorting Queen Elizabeth II on her royal yacht down the newly opened St. Lawrence Seaway to Chicago. During Second-Class (junior) summer, we attended fire-fighting school in Philadelphia; went on an amphibious exercise with the 3d Battalion, 8th U.S. Marines in Little Creek, Virginia; and spent a day under water in a submarine—The Barracuda—off Key West. We took several weeks of flight training at Pensacola, Florida, which included a trip as passengers with the hurricane hunters off the Florida coast, and several landings and takeoffs from an aircraft carrier, the Antietam.

The most important event at the Academy for me, however, occurred Plebe summer, during a meeting with my academic counselor. He informed me I must take a foreign language.

"Do I have to?" I asked.

"Of course, everyone does. What language would you like? Russian, German, Spanish, French, Italian, or Portuguese?"

I realized I knew nothing about foreign languages. After a few moments, I said, "Give me the easiest one of the bunch."

"We'll put you down for Italian."

Foreign language ("Dago" we called it) was the only variable in our curriculum; otherwise, all my classmates took the same courses.

Having survived the summer hazing, we began our academic studies in the fall. The hazing at the hands of upperclassmen continued, but I looked on it as Academy tradition so it didn't change my positive attitude toward becoming a naval officer. My biggest concern soon became my academics, which was a surprise to this confident country boy who had arrived at the Academy with a brilliant academic record. The only subjects that seemed to be going well by the middle of the first semester were History, English, and Italian—not optimum subjects for a school that granted only an engineering degree.

I was amazed at how easily Italian came to me. As I rapidly gained fluency, I found not just satisfaction, but an indescribable pleasure in my ability to express myself as if I were another person, from a different culture. I remember repeating to myself the phrase: "*Italiano è la più bella lingua del mondo*" (Italian is the most beautiful language in the world). It was just so musical!

I would repeat that and other sentences to myself as I sat in my room or marched to classes. During summer training, I practiced my Italian with the Italian immigrants in South Philadelphia. In Pensacola I sought out Italian naval officers for conversational practice. Back at the Academy in the fall of my Youngster (sophomore) year, I frequently volunteered to give speeches at our Italian Club dinners. My professors told me I had a gift. I began to wonder if, perhaps, that might be true. I even began to think and dream in Italian.

The growing contrast of my success in Italian with my struggle in the electrical engineering curriculum, however, became more and more dramatic. And traumatic. I remember one course—college trigonometry—that I was failing for 13 weeks. The fact that I didn't have trig in high school surely played a part, but I also no longer had the interest I thought I would have in mathematics. I failed the final exam, took a re-exam and passed it. Nearly fifty years later, I still have dreams of having to prepare for re-exams.

Although my academic struggles in the technical subjects shocked me, they also increased my fervor for

Italian. I expended more and more time and effort on the language and less and less on my other subjects. At the end of my Youngster year, one of my Italian professors, William Buffum, told me I had gone about as far as I could go in Italian, at least at the Academy. He recommended I take a Slavic or Germanic language next. It so happened that Professor Buffum also taught Russian. He promised that if I learned Russian well, I would always have a job. This was the era of the "Sputnik Scare" and the new national resolve to develop programs in the universities to meet the threat of Communism.

"Italian is a great and beautiful language," he told me, "but not very strategic for career purposes."

As I indicated earlier, in those days, all midshipmen took a rigid program in electrical engineering. (One classmate already had a degree in electrical engineering from Purdue, but he was taking the same courses I was.) There were no variations in individual programs except for foreign language. But foreign languages were offered only for the first two years. In 1960 the Academy began to offer a limited number of electives, some in foreign languages. In order to take them, however, one had to have an overall grade point average of at least 3.3. There was no way I could meet that requirement. So in my Second-Class (junior) year, I found myself with no foreign language classes. I bought a Berlitz book on Russian and began to study it in my room, to the detriment of my other subjects. By the end of the semester I was so far behind in my assigned subjects, it was a foregone conclusion I would bilge out (fail).

Sure enough. In February 1961 I declined the Academy's offer to retake the exams I had failed and, after two and one-half years as a midshipman, walked through Bilger's Gate into the streets of Annapolis. I wasn't discouraged. On the contrary, my energy and ambition would now be channeled in a new direction. I was anxious to move on to the next phase of my life. Somehow or other I was determined to seek a career in foreign languages. I carried with me all sorts of pie-in-the-sky plans. I would find work in Washington, DC, and go to Georgetown University in the fall. My youthful exuberance and naiveté prevented me from considering certain real-life factors, such as gaining acceptance to the university in the first place and, most of all, paying the tuition. At the time, all I thought of was that Georgetown had a good reputation in Russian and Russian was what I wanted to do.

Although in February 1961 I believed I had done the right thing, there were times later in life when I was not proud of the way I left the Academy. I still believe today that it all worked out for the best, but failing courses at the Academy still carries a negative charge in my psyche. In fact, that failure played a crucial role in my later academic success. I was determined to make up for my misguided decision to allow my other studies to fall by the wayside at Annapolis.

CHAPTER 4
MONTEREY

I'd no sooner left Annapolis and arrived in Washington, DC, when reality hit me square in the eyes. The only job I could find was selling encyclopedias. That didn't bring in much money. Although my fiancé from Wisconsin was working in Washington at the FBI, she didn't make enough to pay my way through Georgetown. I found myself preoccupied with making money and living one day at a time. I couldn't come up with a solution that would get me into the university to pursue my study of Russian. In fact, I was so far from being able to afford Georgetown that I didn't even apply for admission.

In the spring of 1961, I met a soldier who had studied Russian at The Army Language School in Monterey, California. His Russian seemed to be very good, and his description of the program there set me to thinking. Might the Army Language School be my solution? But now I found it difficult to reconcile the idea of going back into the service, especially as an enlisted man when I had just been studying to become a naval officer.

Two weeks after my marriage in June, I received a notice from the Naval Reserve informing me that, since I was no longer at the Academy, I was obligated to serve two years on active duty. I could expect orders soon to report to the Navy at the rank of Seaman. That notice tipped the scale. The next day I went to see the Army recruiter.

By July, I was in Army Basic Training at Fort Dix, New Jersey. Things began to look up again. During in-processing, my platoon sergeant asked if there was anyone among us who had previous military training. I said I'd spent two and one-half years at Annapolis. The sergeant pointed at me and said, "You're gonna be the 'Acting Jack,' son." That meant I would wear an armband with sergeant's stripes and work as the platoon sergeant's assistant.

Three weeks later, the platoon sergeant was reassigned to another Army post and the training company commander ordered me to take over his duties. I moved into the platoon sergeant's private cadre room, took over responsibility for platoon training schedules, drilled my platoon, and signed weekend passes for my fellow recruits. One week later I was promoted to "actual" private first class (PFC). So, in addition to my "acting-jack" sergeant's armband, I now also sported a "real" single chevron on my sleeve. I began to get better treatment in the mess hall and barbershop, proving that if a one-eyed man is king in the land of blind men, then a PFC is a big deal in the land of slick-sleeved "buck" privates. Good fortune was smiling on me again.

Photo 8: Private First Class Holbrook, 1961.

Later that month, I found myself crowded into a barracks with more than 100 other anxious basic trainees, all of whom were awaiting with great anticipation our upcoming interviews. For most of us, this was the day we had been looking forward to since we enlisted in the Army. Today we would learn our fate—what specialties we would be trained for and where we would go for advanced schooling.

Outside, both the temperature and humidity were above 90. Inside it was even worse. Cigarette smoke formed a pungent cloud around our heads. But that seemed minor compared to the tension we all felt about our next assignments.

I was particularly uneasy. Two weeks earlier, we'd all undergone a series of aptitude tests as part of the Army's purported attempt to put the right people in the right specialties. Since I was beginning to think that maybe my flunking out of the Academy was a mistake, I decided that from now on, I'd never again "take a dive" on any exams.

The first test of my new resolve came when I took the Army's Morse code aptitude test. As luck would have it, the test was given with a colored light bulb hung in the rafters of the testing building. At Annapolis, Morse code was an intramural sport! Companies would vie against each other to determine who could best send and read light signals, just as we would later do at sea. (In fact, in 1959, during my Youngster cruise in the Atlantic, my buddies and I would talk to each other at night using the signal lights on the bridge of our destroyers. I still have my Morse code training aid from the Academy.) I was very good at it. But now I thought, if I excel on this test, I might be assigned as a "ditty-bopper"—our slang for one who works with Morse code. Still, I'd promised myself never again to fail a test on purpose. I ended up "acing" the Morse code test, but didn't think I'd done too well on the language test. All this was on my mind as I prepared to "negotiate" my assignment with a personnel assignments sergeant.

I'd put all my eggs into one basket. I was determined to pursue my study of Russian. At almost any cost. One of the main reasons I was here stemmed directly from the fact that I couldn't afford to study Russian at a university. I was banking on the Army to help me attain my goal of becoming a Russian linguist. All I needed was for things to continue to go well. If I couldn't study Russian, I had no idea what I'd do.

"Holbrook! You're next," barked the company first-sergeant as he pointed to a wooden field table set up at the end of the room. I took a deep breath and walked over to the table where a personnel sergeant sat shuffling some folders.

"PFC Holbrook reporting, Sergeant."

"Have a seat, Holbrook," he responded without even looking up. After a brief pause, he asked, "What's your first choice of school?" He still hadn't looked up at me.

"The Army Language School. In Monterey. California."

"Fine, but I gotta tell you, that's pretty competitive." He wrote something down, then looked me in the eye. "You might not get the language school. What's your second choice?" He looked down, ready to write my answer on the Army form.

"I don't have a second choice, Sergeant. If I can't go to language school, you can send me to truck-driver school, or make a cook out of me."

The sergeant looked up again and glared at me. "You gotta have a second choice. We don't guarantee nothing. You should know that by now."

He was right, of course. This was 1961, well before the All-Volunteer Army. There were no "contractual agreements" before one signed on the dotted line. I knew full well the Army was infamous for mistraining or misusing its people. They might send someone who had been a draftsman in civilian life to radio school. Or they might train someone in one specialty and then later assign him to some totally unrelated job. I wasn't sure my interview was starting out well. But I couldn't back down. I'd enlisted in the Army with one goal—to go to language school and study Russian. I had to convince this sergeant I was focused only on Russian.

"Well, I don't know what else to say."

"Have it your way. I'm going to put you down for intelligence analyst as a second choice. Now, if you do get to the language school, what language do you want to study?"

"Russian."

"And second choice?"

"It's the same thing, Sarge. Russian's the only language I want."

"What are you? Some kind of smart ass?"

"No, Sarge. It's just that I know what I want to do and that's study Russian in Monterey."

"Fine. But you gotta have two more choices." He hesitated. "So I'll put down Russian, Korean, and German. In that order."

I'd overcome the first hurdle in my efforts to get to Monterey. Later I learned that, in fact, I had barely passed the language aptitude test at Fort Dix. For many years this intrigued me, in light of my future success in foreign languages. The answer to this anomaly came to me some years later, after an assignment at the National Security Agency (NSA). There I helped research and develop aptitude tests. The records of students at NSA, plus my own experience actually teaching Russian in the classroom, showed that a major, to that point undervalued, component of foreign language aptitude was "attitude"— the desire to learn. Since then, it has always been my contention that attitude is the most important factor in predicting future success with foreign languages.

My good fortune continued. Before the end of basic training I received orders to report to Monterey to study Russian. Had my assertiveness with the personnel sergeant actually paid off? In any case I had to admit that, so far, the Army's treatment gave me cause to hope for a rewarding next few years. I'd gone for broke on the Russian language study issue and won.

On my flight to Monterey, I read my first Russian novel—Ivan Goncharov's *Oblomov*. To this day, *Oblomov* remains the only Russian novel I've ever read in English. By the time I got around to my next one, I was reading Russian. *Oblomov* had an immediate and interesting impact on me. The character Oblomov was lazy, while his friend Stolz was very energetic and hard working. By the time my plane landed in San Francisco, I'd finished the book and resolved that from then on, I would emulate the positive, hard-charging Stolz in all that I did.

The learning environment at The Army Language School (later renamed the Defense Language Institute) was ideal. As soldier-students, our main job was to learn a foreign language. Military work details and harassment were kept to a minimum. We spent the first four weeks in the language lab and the classroom learning only one thing: pronunciation. We attended class for six hours a day, five days a week. Our homework usually took three hours each evening. I would go to bed wearing earphones and fall asleep listening to Russian language tapes. My neighbor, a Russian Orthodox priest, graciously allowed me to practice on him and tolerated all my incessant pestering with questions about the language.

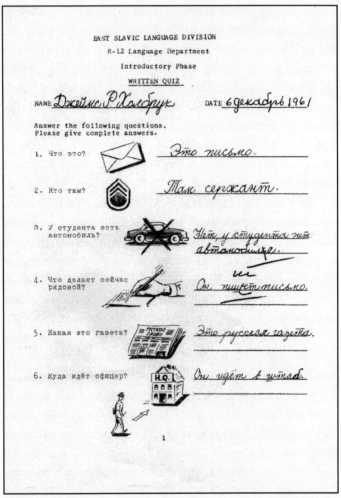

EAST SLAVIC LANGUAGE DIVISION

R-12 Language Department

Introductory Phase

WRITTEN QUIZ

NAME *Джеймс Р. Халбрук*   DATE *6 декабрь 1961*

Answer the following questions.
Please give complete answers.

1. Что это?   *Это письмо.*

2. Кто там?   *Там сержант.*

3. У студента есть автомобиль?   *Нет, у студента нет автомобиля.*

4. Что делает сейчас рядовой?   *Он пишет письмо.*

5. Какая это газета?   *Это русская газета.*

6. Куда идёт офицер?   *Он идёт в штаб.*

1

Photo 9: Top page of my first Russian test at Monterey. The instructor missed a mistake—I used the wrong case when writing the month of December.

In August 1961, I was unaware that USMLM was monitoring Soviet military units on the border of West Berlin or that the East Germans were erecting the Berlin

Wall. We language students went about our business as if nothing was happening. Our studies were so intensive that we were almost oblivious to the outside world.

During the 1962 Cuban Missile Crisis, however, we were not completely out of touch with the world, although little did we realize the U.S. was facing the most dangerous moment in the Cold War. Geraghty cites Paul Johnson, who noted, "Over the Atlantic...were ninety B-52s carrying multi-megaton bombs. Nuclear warheads were activated on 100 Atlas, fifty Titans and twelve Minuteman missiles and on American carriers, submarines and overseas bases. All commands were in a state of 'Defcon-2', the highest state of readiness next to war itself." In October 1962, I was walking to classes in a helmet liner. At school, I was focusing on my reading, in what I thought was the "original," correspondence between Nikolai II and his wife Aleksandra during World War I. (I found out later they had written to each other in French and I was reading a translation.)

After the first three months of my study at Monterey, I was nearly fluent in Russian. By the end of the basic, 12-month course, the Army selected me and four other soldiers for a special advanced class that continued to study for another six months. The closer I got to the end of that course, the harder I worked. By the time I'd finished my studies at the Army Language School, I'd taken a total of 2,250 classroom hours of Russian—roughly equivalent to 25 college semesters (over 12 years) of intensive language study. While at the Language School, I also took a course in Russian history and a course on foreign language teaching at Monterey Peninsula College. (In 1984, I returned to the Defense Language Institute as guest speaker for my son Yasha's graduation from the Russian course.)

When I finished the advanced Russian course, I was scheduled to go either to Shemya, an island in the Aleutian Chain, or to Sinope, Turkey, on the coast of the Black Sea. Both locations were about as close as the U.S. military could get to the Soviet Union for purposes of intercepting Russian communications. Before we left Monterey, however, an alert order came down, and a couple of us were told to stand by for an assignment to the White House Communications Agency. This order delayed our departure for three weeks, while the details of the White House assignment were being worked out. Finally, Washington decided to release us, but meanwhile the Shemya and Sinope assignments had been filled. I received orders to report to West Berlin, Germany—what many called during the Cold War the "Outpost of Freedom." Rather than be near the USSR border, as I would have been at Shemya or Sinope, now I would be surrounded by Soviet troops.

Chapter 5
Teufelsberg, West Berlin

So off to my first intelligence assignment. My wife and I were overjoyed to be going to Europe rather than my going on an unaccompanied tour to the more "exotic" Shemya or Sinope. We left Monterey in May 1963 for leave in Wisconsin. I then went ahead to West Berlin and made arrangements for my wife to follow as soon as I obtained Army approval for her and had found accommodations. (Although my wife was permitted to join me later, I was not yet senior enough in rank to have the Army pay for her travel.) En route to my departure point for the flight to Germany—McGuire Air Force Base, New Jersey—I stopped to visit my Grandfather Kail in Valparaiso, Indiana.

"So, Jimmy, what've you been up to?"

"I'm in the Army, Grandpa. I've been studying Russian."

"Russian? Well, I'll be! *Razumeesh' po-russki?* Do you understand Russian?"

My grandfather immigrated to the United States from Lithuania when he was a young boy. It had never dawned on me that Lithuania was at that time part of the Russian empire. I knew he spoke English with a strong accent, but... Russian?

"*Da, dyedushka. Razumeyu.* Yes, Grandpa, I understand."

"I've forgotten a lot," he said. "My folks smuggled me, Uncle John, and Aunt Bea out when the goddamned Bolsheviks came. But I still remember a few things."

That little bit of information would frequently stand me in good stead later. When suspicious Russians asked why I spoke Russian so well, I would cut the questions short by simply saying, "Well, my grandfather spoke it."

Before reaching Berlin, I had to stop over in Frankfurt for a few weeks of special voice-intercept training at Headquarters, Army Security Agency (ASA), Europe. By then, I'd received a very sensitive security clearance that subjected me to many restrictions. As part of the security indoctrination, personnel from counterintelligence (CI) told all new arrivals that Germany was rife with spies who were working for the Soviets or Soviet-bloc countries. We were ordered to never speak Russian in public. This was hard for me, as I had been speaking it pretty regularly now for nearly two years. Many common, everyday phrases came out automatically.

One evening a buddy and I were in a Frankfurt bar where I let some Russian slip out. Earlier we had been speaking English to the attractive waitress. At the time, my German was limited to "*Ein Bier, bitte*" (a beer, please). The waitress must have overheard us, as she asked if we spoke Russian. I said yes. She then asked if I'd be willing to help her correspond with her sister who resided in East Germany.

"I don't understand. What's the problem?"

"She writes to me in Russian all the time and I don't understand her letters. Would you be willing to translate them for me?"

"Do you have any of them here?"

"No. But you could come over to my place and see them."

Her story made no sense to me. It was obvious to both of us that this was a setup of some kind. Rather than challenge her, however, I told her I'd be happy to translate for her. I never did. In fact, my buddy and I never returned to that bar. I was a little embarrassed that I'd spoken Russian when I shouldn't have, so I didn't report it to anyone. This incident taught me, however, how serious the security threat was in Germany. Just speaking a few words of Russian had led to a possible enemy agent zeroing in on us.

Although I accepted the need for security, nothing in my mind justified one incident I witnessed shortly thereafter. A "raid" of our barracks by Army CI remains vivid in my mind to this day. It must have been about 2 a.m. We were billeted in Gutleut Kaserne, the old Wehrmacht (World War II German military) barracks. Usually, the only noise that penetrated the darkness came all the way from downtown Frankfurt's busy streets. This night, however, we heard a different kind of sound.

The door to our sleeping bay flew open and banged against the wall. Two men barged in.

"Get dressed. You're coming with us," one of them said as he kicked a soldier's bunk.

The lights came on. Everyone in the bay woke up. I shielded my eyes from the sudden light. As my vision gradually adjusted, I saw the two men in civilian clothes standing over the soldier.

The sleepy soldier sat up. "What the hell? Who are you?"

"Never you mind." Both men flashed some kind of badges.

No one said a word while the soldier got dressed and in a few minutes departed with the men in civvies. The rest of us just sat and stared at each other for a few moments. The whole thing had taken place in no more than five minutes. I was the first to say something.

"What the hell just happened?" I asked.

"They were counterintelligence, our CI guys," answered the soldier who occupied the bunk next to mine.

"What do you mean, 'CI guys'? Who the hell are they and what right do they have to come busting in like that in the middle of the night?"

"They're just rounding up Monterey Marys," someone else said.

I'd first heard the term "Monterey Mary" during training in Frankfurt. It referred to linguists who'd been trained at the Army Language School in Monterey. (ASA soldiers who had trained in other specialties at Fort Devens, Massachusetts, were called "Devens Dollies.") While I didn't give it too much further thought, it sounded to me like a derogatory term. But then again, maybe not. After all, I was used to being called a "crab" when I was at Annapolis. Still, some of the guys at work had warned me to be on guard because strange things were happening to linguists. It all sounded so bizarre. I knew I had to watch out for foreign intelligence operatives in Germany, but did I have to watch out for my own people as well?

"Well, I suppose I'm a Monterey Mary," I volunteered with some trepidation, "Are they going to come for me too?"

"Are you a homo?" asked one of my barracks mates.

"A what?"

"Are you a homosexual? A lot of you Monterey Marys are."

"Yeah," said another soldier. "That's what's going on. It's some kind of purge."

The only times I'd ever encountered the word "purge" before was in reference to the Great Purges of the late 1930s in Stalinist Russia. The realization that these men had barged in on us in the middle of night unexpectedly and unannounced—just like the NKVD (the Soviet secret police) had done in Russia—sent a chill up my spine. Things like this were supposed to occur only in the Soviet Union or in other Communist dictatorships.

"And it doesn't matter whether or not you're really gay," one soldier spoke up. "If they think you're gay or that you know someone who is, they'll come after you."

Jesus! I thought. Right out of Soviet history. And this is supposed to be America! Or even if we're in Germany, we're supposed to be treated like Americans.

"Where do they take these guys?" I asked. "What happens to them?"

"I hear they go to some house outside of town where they're interrogated," interjected another of my fellow soldiers.

I couldn't sleep the rest of that night. I had two major fears. One was that they would drag me off just because I was a "Monterey Mary." The other was they might come for me to find out if I knew of any homosexuals among my fellow students at Monterey. My only frame of reference was the Soviet Purges and thinking about them did little to put my mind at ease.

Fortunately, I remained in Frankfurt for only a few more weeks and CI never got around to bothering me. I thought some soldiers from my 12-month course may have been gay, but they were good linguists and they never bothered me, so it was no big deal. I just didn't give it too much thought. Apparently, the "purges" were primarily carried out in Frankfurt. Luckily, I escaped to Berlin without any more encounters with our CI agents.

When I arrived in Berlin in the summer of 1963, World War II had been over for eighteen years. The city was some 110 miles deep in the middle of Communist East Germany. Seven years had passed since the Soviets had "discovered" the Berlin Tunnel that was used to tap Soviet and East German communications. Two years had passed since the Berlin Wall had gone up. A few weeks before my arrival, President Kennedy had visited the city and given his *"Ich bin ein Berliner"* speech.

Scars of the war were still quite visible everywhere. In 1945, Berlin was heavily pounded by American and British bombs, as well as by Soviet bombs and artillery during their Battle of Berlin. After the war, tons of rubble around the city were collected and hauled away to the middle of the nearby Grunewald forest. U.S. and British intelligence commandeered the highest single pile of rubble to set up a listening post where they could monitor Soviet and East German communications. Everyone called our rubble pile "Teufelsberg" (Devil's Mountain). We soldiers and airmen also referred to it as the "Hill" or "T-Berg." In 1963, it was still pretty much a rubble pile.

John Le Carré has described Cold War Berlin as the "eternal city of spies." Personnel security concerns there were even more serious than out in West Germany. This was due, in part, to the fact that when the Soviets pulled out of Austria in 1955, the center of gravity for East-West espionage in Europe shifted from Vienna to Berlin.

The Army Security Agency had been monitoring Soviet and East German communications since 1951 from various locations throughout the city. By July 1961, Teufelsberg became the consolidated site for such operations. In 1963, only a couple hundred officers and men were assigned to our unit. Over the years, however, the organization expanded to more than 1,000 personnel, and in 1967 it was designated Field Station Berlin. Stuart Herrington writes in his book *Traitors Among Us,* that the Soviets considered the ASA SIGINT station on Teufelsberg as "the most dangerous unit." Thus, it became one of the highest priority targets for Soviet espionage in West Berlin. (Years later some notorious spies were indeed recruited by the KGB from the Teufelsberg site.)

In my day, the ASA outfit was called the 78th Special Operations Unit (SOU). We had four 8-hour, rotating shifts called "tricks." One trick would work day shifts for six consecutive days, another would work six "swings," or "eves," and a third would work six "mids"—from midnight to 8:00 a.m. Then, after a 48- or 72-hour break—depending on what the next shift would be—we changed our shift hours. One trick was always on break while the other three worked the revolving schedule.

When I first arrived, only two buildings stood atop Teufelsberg, surrounded by high barbed wire fences. One building housed an array of antennas, while the other had a mess hall. Nearby, we linguists and analysts worked inside mobile Army communications vans that were equipped with desks, banks of tape recorders and radio receivers. A few months later, more semi-permanent structures were built to house our operations.

The ASA listening post no longer exists. Since deactivation of the Field Station, German and Japanese businessmen have proposed building tourist hotels and a ski resort on Teufelsberg. As this book is being finished (2005), part of one operations building, replete with old, deactivated antennas, still stands. Some entrepreneurs want to turn that building into a museum of the Cold War.

Photo 10: Teufelsberg, Berlin. September, 2005.

In 1963, at the age of 23 years, I was no expert on the East-West conflict surrounding Berlin. I knew there was an ongoing Berlin crisis centering on the possibility that the USSR might sign a separate peace treaty with East Germany. That would have made it very difficult for U.S. forces to remain in Berlin. My primary concern, however, was my job—monitoring Soviet communications. I knew nothing about any Berlin-based U.S. Military Liaison Mission.

Counterintelligence told us once that every second person in the city was working for some intelligence service. Of course, that included us soldiers at the 78th SOU. Soviets could travel quite easily back and forth between the four Allied sectors, so one never knew for certain where or when the next KGB or Soviet military intelligence (GRU) officer or their agents might pop up. Still, I was bubbling over with the desire to speak some Russian. As I stated earlier, I'd spoken it almost exclusively over the previous two years. My wife had also learned to speak Russian passably well, so we had used it around the house. My job on the Hill, however, offered no official opportunity to speak the language; I was simply to *listen* to the Soviets. In order to keep up my oral skills, I occasionally spoke quietly to my wife or read softly from my Russian books in our German apartment. I didn't want any of my German neighbors to hear me, so I spoke and read sometimes in a whisper. I'd learned my lesson in Frankfurt.

At work, however, within the secure confines of our vans, mess hall, and our later, new buildings, I tried to speak Russian as much as possible. On mids, when there was little voice activity to intercept, I offered Russian classes to the other soldiers on my trick. Many had only nine months of training at Monterey and very little chance thereafter to practice their oral language skills.

The only public place where I ever spoke Russian was at the Freie Universität Berlin—a new institution established after the war to compensate for the loss of Humboldt University, now over in East Berlin. I was anxious to resume my study of the Russian language and culture, so I registered for an advanced Russian literature course. The course was given in Russian, which was good for me because I spoke no German at the time. All my classmates spoke Russian in class also. Although I never identified myself as a member of the 78th ASA SOU, it must have been obvious to my fellow students that I was a GI. They never questioned me about my background, however, and I received no overtures similar to the one in Frankfurt, so I concluded the security risk was minimal. I also began to study German with a local tutor.

On 22 November 1963, I bought a large Zenith Transoceanic radio because it had not only FM, but also several shortwave and long-wave bands. The Soviets broadcast the Russian-language "Radio Volga"—their equivalent of our Armed Forces Network—on long-wave. That first evening with my new radio I decided to listen to some classical music on a Berlin FM station. I went to bed with the radio playing. The music was very somber. I couldn't understand any of the German, but I did frequently make out the words "John Fitzgerald Kennedy." The next morning, my landlord informed me President Kennedy had been assassinated. While I lay in bed the night of the 22nd, Berliners poured out into the streets, carrying candles in silent tribute to the American president who just months before had been in their city. The next day, Berliners flew their flags at half-mast and wore black; some of them wept on the street. For several days thereafter, Berliners would stop me and other Americans to express their condolences. I recalled how in January 1961, while still a midshipman at Annapolis, I'd trudged through snow and slush in President Kennedy's Inaugural Parade.

Listening in on Soviet military communications at work on the Hill fascinated me. It reminded me of my days as a youth, when telephone service first came to our village. We all shared multiparty lines, each family having a certain number of short or long rings to indicate who the incoming call was for. One of our favorite pastimes as youngsters (the adults did it also) was to take the phone off the hook whenever it rang—no matter for whom the call was intended—and "rubber in" or listen to others' conversations. Now here I was in Berlin, "rubbering in" on Soviet officers and soldiers who were talking about all manner of things. Some conversations were about military matters; others were personal.

A favorite topic among the Soviet soldiers was how many days were left until, and what they planned to do after, *demob* (demobilization)—the day when they would finish their two-year obligation as conscripts (draftees). All soldiers, it seems, count the days remaining until they are to be separated from active duty. But there were many good reasons why that day had a special significance for the Soviet soldier. For example, in the 1970s, young soldiers received barely five dollars a month, which reminded me of Tony Pastor's World War II song about Army pay: "21 Dollars a Day—Once a Month."

Everyday life for a soldier in the Soviet Army was also degrading and dangerous. Soviet parents often wept when their sons went off to active duty. The hazing of new conscripts by older soldiers was often criminal. Although hazing was a violation of Soviet regulations, their officers often looked the other way and insisted their older soldiers (those on active duty for more than six months) were in no way mistreating the new conscripts.

In 2004 I came across an item in the *Denver Post* that stated Russia's chief military prosecutor reported 109 soldiers had committed suicide. That was 38 percent more than during the same period the previous year. The general added that 25 other servicemen were killed in hazing incidents and 12 others died as a result of excess force used by their officers. I've experienced hazing myself—in Navy boot camp and, more seriously, at Annapolis as a Plebe at the Naval Academy. None of that hazing, however, approached the brutality to which young Soviet/Russian soldiers were, and still are, subjected.

Monitoring the conversations of high-ranking officers was often quite entertaining. I soon discovered the higher the rank of the Soviet officer, the less respect he had for what we call "communications security." It often happened that when some general was discussing matters he wasn't supposed to, a female Soviet monitor would break in to remind him he was not to discuss such information over an insecure radio. Then came the almost inevitable rebuke: "Who do you think you are, *devushka* (girl)? Telling a general what he can and cannot say!"

Monitoring and transcribing Soviet military conversations at Teufelsberg were the two primary activities of my military occupational specialty (MOS988). A sub-specialty of that MOS, however, was "imitative communications deception" (ICD). The purpose of ICD is to break into enemy voice communications networks and mislead them with disinformation in one way or another. Such operations are employed generally only in wartime combat situations. (I recall that ICD was used a few times by the Viet Cong against our own forces in Vietnam.) To engage in ICD, one had to be able to pass himself off as a native speaker. The Assistant Operations Officer thought I had that ability, but there was no way to find out for sure, since we were not authorized to break into GSFG communications in peacetime.

One day he devised a plan whereby we would make a tape on which I would play the role of a Soviet soldier discussing a subject of great technical interest to Captain J., our Operations Officer. This captain was recognized as one of the best Russian linguists at our site, at least among the officers. He was also an expert on Soviet radio communications equipment. We made the tape and included just enough static to make it sound like a real, live intercepted conversation. The Assistant Operations Officer then called his boss at home and told him we had intercepted something very interesting. The captain rushed to the Hill. As he listened to the tape, he became very excited and was just about to send out a high-priority message to higher headquarters when his assistant told him the tape was just a hoax—all a practical joke. I'm not sure how much of a joke the captain thought it was, but I had passed the test and there were never any repercussions for me.

Soon I was to get involved in a real-life event that tested my Russian language abilities. This event, I found out many years later, also involved a USMLM rescue mission.

From the 1964 USMLM Unit History, I recently learned that in January 1964, a USAF T-39 twin-engine jet trainer inadvertently flew into the Soviet Zone where the Soviets shot it down. I knew nothing of this incident in 1964. But the Unit History goes on to recount that less than two months later, the Soviets shot down an Air Force RB-66 jet reconnaissance aircraft, also on a training mission, that strayed over the border. A British pilot, flying in the Berlin corridor, reported seeing three parachutes. Although the USMLM rescue teams got close to the crash site, the Soviets prevented them from reaching the crew. It wasn't until six days later that the Soviets informed the Chief of USMLM that one of the pilots had a broken leg and was in a Magdeburg hospital. Eleven days after the shoot-down, the Soviets allowed USMLM to transport the injured airman to West Germany. Seventeen days later, after the intercession of Secretary of State Dean Rusk, the Soviets released the other two officers to USMLM.

In 1964 I knew nothing of USMLM's role in the RB-66 shoot-down. But I too participated in that crisis, possibly as a result of my performance in our earlier successful practical joke.

In the late afternoon of 10 March, the phone rang in my apartment on Neuchateller Strasse.

"Get over to Andrews Barracks immediately," ordered the duty officer at our headquarters. "You'll be going from here straight to the Hill."

"Yes, sir. I'm on my way." I answered. I knew better than to ask over the phone what this was all about. Something had happened or was about to happen and I wouldn't find out any details until I reached the Hill. I threw on my fatigue uniform, jumped into my 1949 Volkswagen and sped off for Andrews. En route I wondered what I'd do if I got stopped for speeding. What would I tell the Berliner Polizei? GIs had certain privileges in West Berlin, but speeding was not one of them.

I made it to Andrews without incident and was told to get into an American MP vehicle. We roared through the compound gate with the siren blaring. When I arrived on the Hill, Captain J., the Operations Officer, met me.

"Come with me, Holbrook."

"What's up, sir?"

"We're not sure yet, but it looks like we have a shoot-down in East Germany."

The captain led me to a rack with tapes and a radio receiver. A soldier who was sitting at the position jumped up when we came in.

"Sit down here," the Operations Officer instructed me. "What we need to know is what happened, where and when and most of all, what's the status of the crew."

"Do you have anything on tape yet, sir?" I asked.

"Yes, of course. But that's not good enough. We need to know immediately, on a real-time basis, what's going on. I'm assigning a couple of runners to stand by here. They'll relay whatever you come up with to the Communications Center. We'll be sending out this information in a series of CRITICs."

CRITIC was our highest message priority and was used only for emergencies. Such reports would be landing on the President's desk in Washington within minutes after being sent from Berlin. It took me a couple of minutes to adjust to the crisis situation and to the Soviets whom I was listening to through my headphones.

"One officer, has a broken leg and is being taken to the Magdeburg hospital," I relayed to the soldier standing next to me. "The other two crewmen are alive and o.k." The soldier ran off to the communications center.

I don't remember a lot of the details from those conversations I heard through that night and the next day and night. I recall, however, the Soviets reported American "missionaries" were being caught and sent to the Gardelegen *komendatura*. I didn't understand what they meant by "missionaries." It was only recently that I learned about the critical role played by USMLM in recovering the downed airmen of the RB-66. I now know that in all likelihood, most of the information I was relaying to the soldiers standing by as runners to the communications center was also being passed to the Chief of USMLM, and may have aided the Mission in its recovery operations.

By the time I was relieved from the listening position, I'd been there for nearly two days. The Soviets were using a multi-channel communications system and I was monitoring 12 different channels. I watched for the telltale spike on the monitor scope that would tell me when a channel became active. If more than one channel became active at the same time, I had to record them and then later listen to the tapes when there was a lull in the Soviets' conversations. My meals were delivered to me and I left my position only to go to the latrine. The Operations Officer asked me several times if I wanted someone to spell me, but my adrenalin level was so high that I had no trouble staying awake and alert. That was my most exciting and rewarding experience at the 78th.

The memory of those two days, and the realization that my Russian skills had enabled me to make a significant contribution during a real live crisis, reinforced my conviction that, where intelligence activities are concerned, rank plays no role. What's important is whether or not you have the skills to meet the challenge. I was then a Specialist Five. My participation behind the scenes of that RB-66 shoot-down incident remains a highlight of my Army career. There would be no shoot-downs or other air emergencies during my time at USMLM.

When I think back about the Soviets' behavior regarding the two shoot-downs, I can see more clearly how the pursuit of intelligence overshadowed diplomatic niceties or even the safety of the flight crews. The Soviet delays in providing U.S. access to the downed aircraft were motivated by their interest in examining the U.S. planes for any intelligence they could glean. We would probably have done the same in their shoes.

In fact, in 1966 a Soviet YAK-28 jet fighter crashed into the Havelsee in the British Sector of West Berlin. Don Cooper writes in his book *A Trick* that "Russian Marys picked up the pilots yelling about going down... We heard them talking all the way down and then nothing, nothing but static. The Russians [ground-based air-controllers] were shitting bricks." British soldiers prevented a Soviet general and a contingent of troops from reaching the scene. The bodies of the two Soviet airmen were returned only two days later. In December 2003, a British documentary revealed that during this incident, the British removed parts of the plane and took them to England for examination. According to Geraghty, those parts were the downed aircraft's engines: "Within forty-eight hours they were flown back to Berlin, 'returned' to the crash site and quietly deposited on the bed of the lake. The day after that, the engines were located officially and publicly by British divers."

A few weeks after the RB-66 shoot-down, during one midnight shift, our Trick Chief, Staff Sergeant Eckford, walked over to where I was working.

"Holbrook, I hear you're pretty good." His tone told me he wasn't being sarcastic.

"Thanks, Sarge. We're all pretty good here."

"What would you think about going back to the States for seven months to take a supervisor's course at NSA?"

"Sounds interesting. Would I get to come back to Berlin?"

"Yeah, of course. Then, when you make staff sergeant, you could become a trick chief."

I need to say a couple of words here about trick chiefs and about the friction that existed between the command element and the operational element at the 78th and probably at all large ASA stations. Many "Monterey Marys" were prima donnas. Most of us were doing our time on active duty and then planning to get out. Several linguists were college graduates, and tended to look down their noses at career soldiers, whom they called "treads" or "lifers." In those days, many of our officers and sergeants were assigned to us from other than Military Intelligence branch. Consequently, they had very little knowledge of what we were doing. They often seemed to be more interested in spit and polish and routine military work details.

We, however, knew our value to the overall operational mission of the 78th SOU. Others knew it also and sometimes encouraged us to be prima donnas. For example, when the Army Chief of Staff, General Harold K. Johnson, visited Teufelsberg, he called the military personnel there, according to Cooper, "technicians and linguists, not soldiers." We sometimes played that card against our command structure when we were dissatisfied with what we considered their interference in our work. Cooper quotes one soldier's response to his trick chief's orders to get a haircut: "You want me to get a haircut or do you want me to do my mother f-ing job? What's it going to be?" There were plenty of exceptions, however, and I hope I was one of them. After all, though I didn't know it at the time, it wouldn't be long before I too would become a "lifer."

Cooper—wittingly or unwittingly—does a great disservice to the Sergeant Eckford I referred to above. Cooper uses Eckford's last name to refer to a platoon sergeant whom, he says, all the ASA soldiers held in contempt. Although perhaps not the same person, Cooper provides a derogatory characterization of a "Sergeant Eckford," a platoon sergeant, who returned to the States and retired.

The real Staff Sergeant Eckford I knew was an infantryman who, initially, knew very little about our operations on the Hill. But Eckford did know how to take care of his men and he learned to appreciate our work. He was also one of the first in a long line of people who gave me some important breaks in my career. After I left the 78th, I next saw him in 1980 as the Command Sergeant Major at NSA—the senior enlisted man in the entire Army cryptologic service at NSA. By then I was a major. Needless to say, we were proud of each other.

Chapter 6
American University

In April 1964, I arrived at NSA, Fort Meade, Maryland, to attend the Russian linguist supervisor course. The first four months of that course consisted of a language refresher. At noon on the first day of class, the school director called me into his office.

"Specialist Holbrook, we don't think you should remain in Russian class. You don't need any refresher training and your presence is disruptive for the others."

"What would I do while my classmates are studying Russian for the next four months?"

"We'd like you to teach a special Russian course for our analysts who don't speak the language, but who come in contact with it every day."

For those four months, I taught several one-week courses at the NSA school. I then rejoined my classmates for the technical supervisor training. When we were about to finish the course, the school director asked if I'd like to stay on as a permanent instructor.

"Does this mean I wouldn't get to return to Berlin?"

"Well, yes. This would be a permanent change of station."

I had a little more than a year to go on my enlistment, our first child had been born the previous July, and I really enjoyed teaching Russian. So I agreed to stay and become a member of the permanent faculty. I taught a wide variety of regular classes. In the evenings, I took college courses in Economics, Russian History, and German language at the University of Maryland Annex at Fort Meade.

In April 1965, my first-sergeant called me in. Almost any soldier, no matter one's rank, tenses up when he or she is ordered to report to the first-sergeant. I could picture myself standing at attention before "Top" and trying to explain something I'd done, or should have done and didn't. When I entered the first-sergeant's office, however, I was relieved somewhat that he offered me a seat.

"Have you ever considered Officer Candidate School (OCS)?"

"Not really, First-Sergeant. If I'd wanted to be an officer and stay in the service, I'd have tried harder to remain at Annapolis."

"You mean you don't plan to stay in the Army?"

"No. I want to go back to school and get my degree in Russian."

The first-sergeant looked at me for a moment, then asked, "Are you aware that the Army sends some soldiers to civilian schooling either to start or to finish their bachelor's degree requirements?"

"No, I've never heard of such a program."

"How much college do you have?

"At least two full years."

"Then you could get your degree in two more, right?"

"Yes, I'm sure I could."

He got up from his desk and pulled from a shelf a large notebook containing Army Regulations. After paging through it, he stopped and handed the open notebook to me.

"See this?"

Sure enough, the Army had a quota of 120 soldiers per year to be detailed to civilian universities for study in various fields that would be useful to their military specialties.

"You think you might want to apply for this?"

"You bet, First-Sergeant."

"You'd have to reenlist for six years. The Army requires two additional years of service for every year in the program."

That stopped me short. First, I'd had reservations about enlisting in the Army in the first place until I got the threatening Naval Reserve call-up alert. Then I'd had to extend that initial Army enlistment for 11 months to be eligible for the advanced course in Monterey. Now I would have to serve even longer. But look what I would be getting out of it. A college degree in Russian! I decided to go for it.

It didn't take me long to fill out the application and within a few weeks I was accepted into the program. I would become a fully matriculated student for two years at The American University (AU) in Washington, DC. I'd draw my full pay and the Army would take care of all tuition and books.

Before I departed Fort Meade for AU, I was called before a promotion board. They too were interested in whether I'd like to go to OCS. I respectfully declined and told them of my upcoming opportunity to study at AU.

"Then perhaps we shouldn't promote you to staff sergeant," threatened one of the board members. "You've been in the Army only three and a half years and maybe you're getting pretty satisfied with yourself."

In June 1965, Staff Sergeant Holbrook began his studies at AU. At the end of that summer, I received yet another big break. After the summer sessions, the Department Chairman Vadim Medish asked me to present my transcript from Monterey and take a placement test. After the department evaluated all my work at the Language School, AU awarded me 40 credit hours, which essentially covered all my academic major requirements. I now had only to spend a semester of residence, take a couple other courses, and I would meet all requirements for my Bachelor of Arts in Russian.

After receiving my BA in January (graduating in the top third of the class of 1966), I had one and one-half years yet to go on the Army-sponsored civil-schooling program. I requested and was granted permission by the Army to remain at AU and pursue a Master's degree. American University was chartered initially as a graduate school. It catered to the needs and schedules of the many government workers in Washington. Consequently, all graduate courses were held in the evening, so my days were free for homework or other activities.

During the next year and a half, I took graduate courses and focused on a contrastive analysis of English and Russian grammar. I wrote my Master's thesis in Russian on a particularly complex Russian verb category for English speakers: verb aspect. At AU all my courses were on the Russian language, Slavic and English Linguistics, and Russian literature. My only courses conducted in English were on English-language linguistics.

Being young and energetic, and once again being in a Russian linguist's "hog heaven," I took advantage of my classes being only in the evening. I began to participate in several additional activities. For a while, I substitute-taught Russian and German at some local high schools. At AU, I taught a Russian basic course and published and edited a Russian-language newspaper. I taught grammar and written Russian to a young lady who spoke the language fluently, but who couldn't read and write. I also tutored a gifted young boy in Russian. In addition, I wrote and produced with two other students a Russian-language radio program on WAMU-FM. On the air, the three of us were Yasha, Sasha, and Masha. I was Yasha.

I received the nickname "Yasha" from Professor Medish. Yasha is the diminutive of Yakov, the biblical name for James. It is not unusual for foreign language students to adopt names from the culture whose language they're studying (my granddaughter Jennifer uses the name "Isabel" when she writes to me in Spanish.) Since I took so many Russian courses at AU, the name Yasha became a regular part of my daily life. Subsequently, it was a name I continued to use among colleagues, other Russian specialists, and Russian friends for the next several years. (In 1967, when I arrived at my assignment in Vietnam, my battalion operations officer asked me what name I went by. When I suggested "Yasha," he said, "I ain't gonna call you no goddammed Communist name." For the rest of my tour with the battalion, he called me "Vladimir"!) Since I spoke only Russian to my children for their first few years, I named my first son James but have called him Yasha ever since. In fact, today he is known to almost everyone, including his co-workers and his wife, as "Yash." I rarely use my Yasha nickname anymore. Michael, my youngest son, I call Misha. My daughter's name is Tarisa. Perhaps I should have nicknamed her Tasha.

Photo 11: The author as a staff sergeant and graduate student at The American University, 1966.

By the spring of 1967, I was looking forward to receiving my MA in Russian and returning to uniformed duty. I was hoping to get back to West Berlin and was planning to apply at the first opportunity for promotion to Linguist Warrant Officer. To me warrant officer was the ideal rank for someone who was as engrossed in the language as I was. Also warrant officer rank would guarantee me Russian-language assignments for the rest of my career if I chose to stay in. As a warrant officer, I also knew I would be more inclined to make the Army a career.

I made some preliminary inquiries about the possibility of becoming a warrant officer, but found there were no vacancies in my military specialty at that time. Instead, on the recommendation of my first-sergeant at Military District Washington Headquarters, I applied for a direct commission to officer rank. Initially, I wasn't especially keen on becoming an officer. Besides, the pay for a second lieutenant wouldn't have been much better than what I was already getting. But there were other considerations I had to take into account.

Mainly, there were great assignments in the Army as a commissioned officer Russian specialist that I wouldn't be eligible for as an NCO. Furthermore, when I entered the Army's civilian schooling program, I had taken on that six-year active-duty obligation. I still had four more years to go. By getting commissioned, my obligation would be reduced by two years.

Again on the recommendation of my first-sergeant, I applied for a commission at the rank of captain, based on my six years service, my current rank of staff sergeant, and my Master's degree. Major Jim Teal at the Military Intelligence (MI) Personnel Branch promised to do what he could, but was pessimistic about my being advanced directly to captain. On 4 June 1967, I received my MA. The next day I was sworn in as a first-lieutenant in Military Intelligence. One year later, in Vietnam, I was promoted to captain.

Chapter 7
Vietnam

From American University I moved on to a three-month course for new officers at Fort Devens, Massachusetts, the Army Security Agency school center. This gave me a chance to adjust to my new rank (and to learn how to put officer insignia on my uniform correctly!) From there I was scheduled to go to Korea for a year. It was part of the payback, I guess, for getting the commission.

I wasn't looking forward to Korea, as I would be separated from my family during that time and, besides, I didn't speak Korean. One of my fellow officers in the course had orders for South Vietnam. He was a product of the Army's Reserve Officers Training Corps (ROTC) and was doing his two years of active duty. He then planned to return to civilian life. For my part, I had begun to think I might stay in the Army and knew that if I did, I would have to go to Vietnam sooner or later. We decided to ask Military Intelligence Branch to switch our assignments. They approved the change in our orders, so in November 1967 I arrived in Saigon.

During the first half of my tour in Vietnam, I served as the ASA Liaison Officer to Lieutenant General Fred Weyand's Second Field Force Headquarters, Vietnam (IIFFV). It was a heady experience hobnobbing with senior officers after having been a staff sergeant only a few months earlier. General Weyand's 6'5" height and nine stars!—three on each collar and three on his cap—made quite an impression on this 5'6" new lieutenant.

After his first day back from R&R, General Weyand's staff gave him an overall update briefing. Then the general sent all the officers out of the room, except the Special Security Officer, Major Ben Anderson, and me. Major Anderson brought him up to speed on the special intelligence situation. When Anderson finished, General Weyand turned to me and said, "What do you think, Lieutenant?" I jumped to my feet and said something about Major Anderson having covered everything but that my battalion was watching the Viet Cong (VC) communications situation very closely and we would probably have new information each day. The general nodded his head, stood up, and before leaving the room shook my hand and said, "Welcome aboard." If I handled myself well on that occasion, I could thank my training in Toastmasters International. Our Toastmaster meetings regularly tested us with what we called "table topics"— impromptu two-minute talks on topics assigned without warning. We quickly learned to think on our feet at a moment's notice.

Our Army in Vietnam had little need for Russian. It was the only period in my nearly 30-year career where I didn't work in some Russian-language or Soviet-related field. Still, before my year in Vietnam was up,

I used Russian twice in an official capacity. During the interrogation of two North Vietnamese officers, I was called in to verify that they spoke Russian, since they stated they had been trained in the Soviet Union. They were probably telling the truth, as they did speak Russian. (During my last six months in Vietnam, I spoke Russian with an enlisted man in my detachment who had graduated from the language school in Monterey and spoke Russian quite well.)

I had no problem being in a non-Russian assignment since I believed during wartime it was important for all Army officers to serve in the war zone. In fact, I was glad to be there. I remembered my disappointment at not being old enough to serve in the Korean War. I knew some of the older men in the DeSoto area who had served in World War II and Korea. They talked about it all the time. Although they sometimes spoke of its horror, their stories also contained a nostalgia that increased over the years. They viewed their time spent in the Pacific, Europe, or Korea as a badge of honor. According to them, war had made them "tough" and "proud." It had been the life-defining moment for many of them. I figured I would have missed an important life experience if Vietnam had not come along. I hoped I would be up to the challenge.

I traveled by jeep and helicopter to all the divisions and ASA units in the corps zone. It was my first experience with the use of signals intelligence (SIGINT) in combat. At night, back in my "hootch" (living quarters), I would scan the airways on my short-wave radio, trying to find Soviet communications. We knew there were Soviet advisors in North Vietnam, but I was never able to intercept any conversations. (A Soviet officer I would meet during my tour at USMLM, and later in my career, had been a Soviet advisor in North Vietnam at the same time I was in South Vietnam.)

Until January 1968, it was quiet in our base camp area. There were a few ammo dumps blown up on the periphery, but there were no VC or North Vietnamese (NVA) attacks on our compound. On the evening of 30 January, however, things changed dramatically.

During the previous few weeks, ASA intelligence had concluded there would soon be countrywide attacks on American forces. Near midnight on the 30th, my battalion operations officer rousted me from my bunk.

"Get up, Vladimir. You gotta get some urgent information to General Weyand."

When I got dressed, he handed me a written report.

"Read this when you get to the Headquarters. Then give it to Weyand."

When I knocked on the door to the general's hootch, I knew the information I had would justify waking him up. Our analysts expected countrywide attacks to begin at any moment. The general was in his pajamas. He sat down on a couch in his living room and read the report.

"Just take a seat," he said. "In case I have any questions."

"Yes sir." As a liaison officer, all I knew was what was in the report, so I was sure I wouldn't be able to amplify any of the information. But I could certainly take his questions back to my battalion for answers. The general seemed satisfied with the completeness of the report and immediately got on the phone with his division commanders. He contacted the 11th Armored Cavalry

Regiment in Cu Chi and ordered one squadron to head immediately for Saigon.

"That's all, Lieutenant. Keep me posted if you get anything else. Looks like we're going to have a busy night."

I set out to return to my battalion. Before I reached my own headquarters, the sky in the distance lit up with artillery and gunship fire. When I arrived back at battalion, I went to bed, but not to sleep. I wondered what was really going to happen. I hadn't been in my bunk an hour when our battalion came under fire from VC or NVA artillery.

Incoming rockets exploded near enough to rattle my building and knock the light fixtures out of the ceiling. The Tet Offensive had begun. I rolled onto the floor, pulled my mattress over me and crawled under the bunk. When the first salvo of rockets stopped, I quickly crawled out from under the bunk, donned my helmet and flak jacket, threw on my boots, grabbed my pistol belt, and raced outside.

Running at full speed in my skivvies toward the battalion headquarters bunker, I suddenly found myself sprawled flat on my face. Momentarily stunned, I felt a burning pain in my left knee, but didn't yet know what had hit me. As I jumped up and collected my helmet, I saw blood all over the lower half of my left leg. I also saw the gravel pile with which I had collided in the dark. But I could still run.

Several other officers from the battalion staff came running into the bunker. Someone pulled the door shut and everyone sat in silence, breathing hard. We could hear gunfire and shouts outside. A voice could be heard yelling, "They're inside the perimeter!" Long machine gun bursts seemed to be getting closer, but there was no way we could tell whether it was friendly or enemy fire. The battalion commander soon became hysterical.

"They're getting closer! They're getting closer! We're going to die!" the colonel cried out in a surprising falsetto. I knew at any moment a Viet Cong soldier could open the bunker door and throw in a hand grenade. Why hadn't they thought to put an inside lock on the door? Maybe the colonel was right. For the first time in my life I actually believed I might die in the next few minutes. But with each passing hour, the fighting sounded farther and farther away. As my sense of personal safety grew, I felt both relief and shame. This was not what war was supposed to be like. How many times, in all the World War II movies I had seen, did officers huddle together in a command bunker?

At daybreak, the ferocious Cobra helicopter gunships that had recently arrived in country did exactly what was expected of them. Unable to operate at night, they now lifted off and scattered or annihilated the enemy.

As I stumbled out of the bunker into the bright sunlight, I saw my leg was covered with dried blood. I made my way to the medical point. Triage shunted me aside and I sat for two hours before being attended to by a medic.

Son-of-a-bitch! I thought. How embarrassing to be here just because I didn't look where I was going. Deep down I admitted to myself I had wanted to get "slightly" wounded. I recalled something Hemingway said about what a satisfying feeling it was to get wounded—"getting beat up for a good cause." But falling flat on one's face was not exactly "getting wounded." When my turn finally came, the medic removed some gravel pebbles from my knee, put some antiseptic on it, and sent me back to battalion.

Four days after the attack, the battalion commander called me into his office. The colonel had regained his composure.

"Headquarters sent down a list of individuals who were treated at the medical point after the attack the other night. Your name's on it. The only one from our battalion. Where were you wounded?"

"Ah, er... I wouldn't really call it a wound, sir. I tripped over a gravel pile on my way to the bunker and scraped my knee."

"Well, you still needed medical treatment. And this is war. We need someone in the battalion to get a medal. I'm recommending you for the Purple Heart."

A part of me wanted to say "Thank you, sir" and leave. What a lucky break. It was all legal. The colonel had a good point: if there hadn't been an attack, I wouldn't have run into the gravel pile that night. And a Purple Heart would go a long way towards overcoming my "headquarters' weeney" image. Maybe no one would ever ask how and where I was wounded.

But there was something not quite right here. Could soldiers get a Purple Heart for just being in the wrong place at the wrong time? Yes. The medal was for wounds, not heroism. But by just being spastic? Besides, when I thought of how Hemingway exaggerated, even lied, about his wounds in Italy, I recalled how much respect I had lost for the great American macho hero. And Faulkner... he lied even more about his so-called wounds during World

War I. He never even made it to the war zone! He spent his whole time as an aviation cadet in Canada! Still, a Purple Heart would be proof I had been injured in a war zone. But what's that got to do with being clumsy and not watching where you're going?

"Well? Are you gonna just stand there? Don't you have anything to say?"

"Yes sir. I'd rather you didn't recommend me. Actually, my wound is a little embarrassing."

"It could help your career. And make the battalion look good."

"Yes, I know, sir. But if it's all the same to you..."

"Suit yourself, Lieutenant."

I left the commander's office with mixed feelings. But my conscience was clear. Later I learned about a general who was shot in the ear and (justifiably) received a Purple Heart. He wrangled a medical evacuation back to Washington and then sent a message to his former unit requesting he be recommended for a Silver Star, which he subsequently (unjustifiably) received. A few months after Tet, the officer I was replacing as a unit commander advised me that if I provided a case of C-rations to the commander of the South Vietnamese military intelligence unit, the latter would see to it I received the South Vietnamese Medal of Honor! I passed up that opportunity also and came home from Vietnam with a few less medals, but with a clear conscience.

Fighting associated with the Tet Offensive continued in the area for nearly six weeks. I once had to crawl to the mess hall on my stomach because someone was shooting at me from across the road. Immediately after the first wave of attacks, communications were severed between our battalion headquarters and our analysis and processing company at Bien Hoa Air Base. That meant we had no intelligence information to pass on to IIFFV. As the liaison officer there, I felt it my duty to do whatever was necessary to get that information. I volunteered to go in an armored personnel carrier (APC) across the area where remnants of North Vietnamese regiments were still ensconced. As we prepared to depart our battalion area, I decided I'd rather not ride inside the APC, which I believed was an ideal target for an anti-tank round. I took up a position on top of the vehicle and we traveled, heavily armed, but without incident, the few miles to Bien Hoa. My first Bronze Star was awarded for that "feat."

When Tet Offensive activities had died down, the battalion commander gave me a few days to take in-country R&R. I hitchhiked by helicopter and airplane south to the Vung Tao resort area along the eastern coast. The first night there, I stayed with a Navy SIGINT unit whose quarters were in a cave. It was so unbearably quiet that night that I had trouble getting to sleep. The next day I moved to a hotel in the city. Vung Tao was a no-fire zone. Consequently, I spent a few days lounging on the beach side-by-side with other American soldiers and sailors... and Viet Cong soldiers who also were taking some R&R. The only signs that a war was going on were the sounds from B-52 bombs exploding in the distance.

Photo 12: The author with Army helicopters, 1967.

During the second half of my tour in Vietnam, I commanded an ASA Detachment assigned to the 199th Light Infantry Brigade. By the time I arrived at the 199th, most of the after-effects of the Tet Offensive had disappeared. The 199th continued to conduct combat operations, primarily south of Saigon, in the northern part of the Mekong Delta. No more countrywide attacks took place until after I left Vietnam in November 1968.

For security reasons, ASA units were called radio research units. My command was of the 856th Radio Research Detachment. When I was at IIFFV headquarters, I was required to wear Signal Corps insignia. At the 199th, I wore Infantry crossed rifles. I never understood the reasons for pretending SIGINT units and personnel were not in Vietnam. In fact, military intelligence personnel who were not engaged in SIGINT wore MI insignia. I guess it was one of the fictions of the war—the VC and

North Vietnamese supposedly didn't know U.S. Forces were conducting SIGINT operations.

The priority tasking for my unit in support of the 199th was target acquisition, something we did primarily with radio direction finding (RDF). I traveled back and forth between our main base camp in Long Bihn and the forward command post in the south. My RDF teams were distributed at artillery fire support bases (FSBs), together with combat units of the 199th. Visiting them presented me with an even closer look at combat intelligence. During all my travels to the Mekong Delta area and to the FSBs, I was shot at, had a few near-collisions in helicopters and some close calls with friendly artillery, but never again got "wounded."

I returned home feeling, like many who survive their war experiences, relieved but a little guilty to have made it while so many of our comrades did not.

CHAPTER 8
GEORGETOWN AND WEST POINT

Soviet-related work awaited me again in November 1968 when, after Vietnam, I joined the Army Chief of Staff's Intelligence Support Branch at the Pentagon. There, at the Soviet desk, I followed high-level, strategic political-military developments in the USSR and helped prepare a special, all-source intelligence "black book" briefing each morning for the Secretary of the Army, the Chief and his principal staff officers.

Within a few months, my active-duty obligation would end. My plans at that point were to leave the Army and use the GI Bill to resume graduate school in Russian. For any non-government career in Russian, I believed a doctorate was an absolute prerequisite. My MI career counselor, Major Jim Teal—the officer who helped me get my direct commission and who'd also been to Vietnam and back by then—called me to ask whether I would consider extending my active-duty tour.

"No sir. I'm hoping to return to school on the GI Bill." I explained to him the need for a PhD in order to be hired by any university. He said he understood. The next day he called me back and said there was an authorization in military intelligence for an officer to pursue a PhD in mathematics.

"No, that's not what I had in mind, sir. First of all, I've already had two years of civilian schooling."

"Ah, yes. But that's when you were enlisted. As an officer you're eligible to do it again."

"The second thing is that mathematics is not my forte." I pointed out to him that it was mathematics and related subjects that got me in trouble at Annapolis. "I appreciate your effort to help me out, but I'm afraid I have to decline."

Still, I began to think about the logistics and costs of returning to graduate school. This time my planning benefited from a little more circumspection. This time, at least, there was the GI Bill. I could work somewhere part-time or perhaps get a teaching assistant's position at the university where I would be studying.

Once again, Lady Luck intervened. Major Teal called again and told me he had been in contact with the U.S. Military Academy at West Point. He pointed out they often send their future faculty for graduate schooling. Was I interested?

I quickly said, "Yes!"

Shortly thereafter, I received a call from the Head of the Foreign Language Department at West Point, Colonel Walter Renfroe, who asked me to come up for an interview. When I entered his office he had spread out before him my military service record and my transcripts from the Naval Academy and The American University.

"I see you had some difficulties at Annapolis."

"Yes sir. I was in over my head in engineering subjects."

"But you made it for two full years. What happened your Second-Class year?"

"When my Italian class was taken away, I guess I just felt trapped. A duck out of water. I was already thinking of leaving the Academy. But you know how that goes."

In those days, there was tremendous pressure to keep cadets and midshipmen at the academies after they had completed two years of government-financed education. Today they are not allowed to leave the academies at will, without financial penalties.

"Yes, of course." He paused as he looked over my other transcripts. "But I see you had no troubles at American. Almost straight A's."

"Yes sir. I think I've found my niche in life. I intend one way or another to continue with my Russian."

He sat back and gazed at me for a moment. "We would like to have you teach Russian here at West Point."

"That'd be great, sir."

"But we have no vacancies here for two years. How would you like to go to graduate school until then?"

"Where do I sign, sir?" I could hardly restrain myself. The colonel smiled.

"We'll make arrangements to set you up at a university. As soon as you tell us where you want to go."

"I can tell you right now, sir. Georgetown. I've always wanted to go there, and since I already live in the DC area, there would be no need for the Army to move my family and me. I'm sure I can gain admission, based on my work at American."

By June 1969, I was a doctoral student at Georgetown. My course work there was also exclusively in Russian and Slavic Linguistics, Theoretical and Applied Linguistics, and Russian literature. Here I was able to delve deeply into the language, taking courses on the history of Russian and Old Church Slavonic—the "Latin" of the Slavic world. Later, in the USSR, I would be able to read Old Church Slavonic inscriptions inside cathedrals and on icons that were often unintelligible to many Russians. By the summer of 1971, thanks to this second Army scholarship, I had finished my doctoral course work at Georgetown. I planned to take my comprehensive exams and write my doctoral dissertation during the next three years, while assigned as an instructor and assistant professor of Russian at West Point.

Not counting my year in Vietnam and my assignment in Berlin, my first ten years in the Army had been spent almost entirely in schools where I'd studied Russian language and related subjects. I'd acquired considerable knowledge of Russian history and culture. Still, for the most part, that was all "book learning." I had not yet been to the Soviet Union and I'd had very little interaction with Russians who lived there. My tour in Berlin had given me only passive, indirect contact. Before taking up my teaching duties at West Point in the fall, I convinced my friend Dexter Dickinson—another Russian speaker, a fellow graduate student at Georgetown, and an old army buddy—to join me for a two-week Pan Am tour to Moscow, Leningrad, Kiev, and Sochi.

The Army gave me permission to travel to the USSR, apparently because I had been away from intelligence work for some time. My request was approved with the proviso that I get a security briefing before I departed. I reported to the CI office in the Pentagon and was given some papers to read. The individual in charge of my briefing warned me that I would be "dealing with Communists" as soon as I got to the USSR. He made no mention of reporting back to his office when I returned. Since nothing untoward occurred in the USSR, I made no report and CI never contacted me about the trip.

In late May 1971, Dex and I sat in the Dulles International Airport waiting area, nervous, excited, but more than ready to board an Aeroflot plane to Moscow. We had heard strange stories about Aeroflot flights, but the price was so much lower than on Western airlines that we decided to be adventurous. Besides, essentially, we would be in the Soviet Union the moment we stepped onto the Aeroflot plane.

"Let's promise each other we'll speak only Russian for the duration of this trip," Dex suggested.

"Sounds good to me. The more we try to 'go Russian' the better. I've not even brought any American pipe tobacco with me."

Dex, who also smoked a pipe, raised his eyebrows, then frowned. "Well, I don't know if I'd go that far. I brought along several packages of Half-and-Half tobacco."

We arrived in Moscow at night and went straight to our room in the new Rossiya Hotel. The next morning, I was up early and stepped out for a smoke. No one but the doorman seemed to be about yet.

"Good morning," I said to him in Russian. He returned the greeting nonchalantly.

"What's the weather going to be today?"

"The devil only knows." Maybe, I thought, Russians don't talk about the weather.

"I'm with an American tour group. We hope to visit the Kremlin today."

"*Khorosho*"(good) was his only reply. Obviously I wasn't going to get a very lively conversation out of the doorman who had probably been up all night.

I scanned the horizon for KGB, but saw no one. I was, after all, an American military intelligence officer. Did the Soviets know this? I indicated on my visa application that I was an army officer, but listed my duties as "Assistant Professor of Russian at West Point." No mention of my being in intelligence. I decided to walk down to the end of the building, keeping the front door and the doorman in sight at all times. Still, no sign of surveillance. There was no one out walking, although a car passed from time to time.

I took a deep breath and turned the corner. Now I was isolated, beyond the view of the doorman. I stopped and puffed on my pipe for a few minutes, continually checking to see if anyone was watching me. Then I proceeded to walk around the entire hotel. I made it safely back to the main entrance without being kidnapped and thrown into the Lubyanka prison. It seems rather comical now, in retrospect, but the case of Yale Professor Frederick Barghoorn was in the back of my mind. He had been snatched off a sidewalk in front of his hotel by the KGB and exchanged later for a Soviet spy the United States was holding. Not that I would have been of any value, but I believed anything could happen once you were on Soviet territory.

To be safe, I wanted to make sure the American Embassy knew Dex and I were in the Soviet Union. The first morning, I reported into the Defense Attaché Office (DAO) at the embassy and gave them a copy of our itinerary.

Despite my not being kidnapped outside the hotel in Moscow the first morning of our visit, I remained on guard for any Soviet intelligence service provocations. When our primary guide Zhenya asked what I did, I told him I was an army officer who taught Russian at West Point. When he asked what my branch of service was, I said "Military Intelligence." He raised his eyes and said, "Oh, *shpion* (a spy)?" I countered with what I thought was only a slightly misleading answer: "No, my training is in combat intelligence, reconnaissance for combat operations." Whether or not he knew ahead of time that I was an intelligence officer, I'll never know. But I saw no reason for lying about my status at that time. I was already there in the USSR and the chances were good they had me in their files somewhere.

A few days later, in Kiev, our local guide, a young attractive Ukrainian woman, Mila, paid particular attention to me. One day she pulled me aside and asked if there was anything she could do for me.

"What do you mean?"

"Well, just anything. You're obviously very interested in our country. I'd be happy to do something special for you."

"We have a pretty busy schedule already," I said.

"You do have some free time. Perhaps I can show you some special sights."

The man in me said "Very interesting. Where might this lead?" The intelligence officer in me said "Look, you dope. Can't you see this is a setup?" I decided to play the naive tourist.

"Well, there is one thing I'd like to do, but it might not be possible."

"What's that? I can do just about anything." She smiled at me.

"I'd like to see a library," I said. "We've not seen any in the USSR."

She continued to smile at me, but the smile changed somewhat. She hesitated for a moment and then said, "I'll see what I can do."

The next morning the entire group toured the Ukrainian State Library. Some of the other people in our tourist group complained about this change in schedule, but, if my earlier suspicions had been correct, I felt I had won a small victory over the KGB.

Dex and I learned several things during those two weeks. We got a feel for the rhythms of the people, the way shopping worked, how traffic was controlled, how people dressed. In Leningrad, I spent an evening in my hotel talking to an old woman who had lived through the Siege of 1941-44.

We learned lessons one doesn't find in a textbook—for example, that items on a restaurant menu were often not available and one could not get borscht just everywhere. The nicest souvenirs were available only in special stores set up for foreigners, where dollars or other hard currency was required. Entrance fees to museums and art galleries were set much higher for foreigners than for Soviet citizens. Public transportation was inexpensive, but while busses, trolleys and the famous Moscow Metro took you to just about any interesting point in the city, one had to get used to being packed in like sardines. Dex and I had to push to get on and jockey for position to get off. I learned one other personal lesson: Russian tobacco was not really acceptable to my fine-tuned Western taste. I swallowed my pride a few days into the trip and asked Dex if he would share his Half-and-Half with me.

One very important professional observation for me was that Russians didn't speak the language the way it was portrayed in textbooks. I decided to give this subject more attention when I returned to West Point. Later in the academic year at the Academy, during a Russian literature course I taught, the cadets came to me and complained about the language in some Soviet stories. "We've looked up every word and understand them all, but when they're put together in these sentences, they don't make sense," they told me.

The more I studied the issue, the more I realized that actual speech, even by educated Russians, was phonologically and structurally different from the written language or the language contained in all American Russian-language textbooks. Hence the subject I chose for my doctoral dissertation, which I wrote while teaching at West Point: "Linguistic Peculiarities of Colloquial Russian and Their Role in Teaching Russian." I tested some of my conclusions on my cadet students. Little by little they began to understand contemporary Russian literature better.

Teaching gave me a great sense of accomplishment. To watch someone who arrived in class knowing not a single word of Russian and then after only two years of study be able to carry on a respectable conversation was a wonderful experience. And what a way to multiply one's own expertise—by sending motivated and qualified students out into the world! I began to wonder if I should apply for the West Point Permanent Associate Professorship (PAP) in Russian and Chinese. The PAP position would come open in the next few years.

In spring 1972, I passed my written and oral comprehensive exams and turned immediately to writing my doctoral dissertation. I made monthly trips to Georgetown to meet with my mentor, Professor Anatoly Flaume. One summer, I roomed in a university dormitory, while I continued to do research and write. By late summer 1974, I successfully defended my dissertation and completed my tour at West Point. I was now about to reenter the intelligence world.

Photo 13: Faculty of the Department of Foreign Languages, USMA, West Point, 1972. The author is in the front row, far left. Majors Rich Kosevich and Ed Hamilton, both of whom served later at USMLM, are: fourth row, second from left; and last row, first on left, respectively.

**Photo 14: Two of my children, Yasha and Tarisa,
holding a banner we had taken to the Army-Navy game
in 1972. The Russian translates as "Beat Army!" I've
never lost my loyalty for Navy sports.**

Prior to returning to intelligence—an activity that
would mean security and travel restrictions again—I
decided to go back to Moscow for a short trip with my
wife. Once again, I went through official channels by
requesting permission to make the trip. After another
superficial "security briefing," we left for the Soviet Union.
When I returned from Moscow, CI failed to contact me
about my trip. Twice now, in three years, a U.S. military
intelligence officer had traveled to the USSR and CI had
not demonstrated the slightest interest.

During the second Moscow trip in 1974, I paid
particular attention to the speech patterns of the Russians.
The syntactic variations that educated Russians employed
in their speech reinforced my belief that my dissertation
had been "on the money."

On that second trip to Moscow I ran into an Assistant Naval Attaché, Lieutenant Commander Dick Life, who had been a classmate of mine at Annapolis. We went to dinner at Dick and Sandra's apartment and the more we talked the more I began to consider applying for the position of attaché in Moscow.

Now I had two conflicting goals. One was to apply for the PAP position at USMA. That would take me out of the mainstream Army. I would remain at West Point until I completed thirty years service or, if I were later appointed full professor, until I was 65 years old. The other idea beginning to capture my imagination was to attempt to get assigned to Moscow as a military attaché. At one point during my West Point tour, a U.S. Assistant Army Attaché in Moscow was declared *persona non grata* and was required to leave the USSR. Lieutenant Colonel William Odom, for a short time my neighbor at West Point but at the time stationed in Moscow, wrote and suggested I apply to be the replacement since I was already well trained in the language. I discussed this possibility with my MI Branch Chief and Major General Aaron, then the Assistant Chief of Staff, Intelligence, on the Army Staff. They decided it was best for me to continue where I was. An attaché position would always be a possibility for the future, they told me.

CHAPTER 9
GET YOUR STEEL TEMPERED

One more school remained before I returned to intelligence work. The Military Intelligence Officer Advanced Course at Fort Huachuca, Arizona, was designed to train MI captains of all intelligence specialties in the formalities and procedures of intelligence staff work—to provide the big picture. Advanced courses were the highest level of schooling for captains in all the Army's branches. The Infantry had one, Artillery had one, and so on. The next step in professional military education would be staff college, but not all officers would get that opportunity, as staff college involved a competitive selection process.

Several future scenarios vied for my attention while I studied at Fort Huachuca. Chances were good that I would be assigned to Germany after completing the Advanced Course. I began to study German again, this time on my own. After my last tour in Germany, I resolved to know the language before I returned there. Additionally, I bought tapes and books and began studying Chinese with a couple in my Advanced Course who were Chinese-Americans and who spoke Mandarin fluently. The Permanent Associate Professor position at

West Point was still in the back of my mind. I also took some Arabic lessons from a Jordanian officer whom I sponsored at the school.

Toward the end of our course at Fort Huachuca, we held our class's formal dinner—called a "dining-in" in the Army. We invited the Army's Assistant Chief of Staff for Intelligence, Major General Harold Aaron, out from Washington, DC, as our guest speaker. I was class leader, therefore, "president" of the dining-in. During the evening, I again brought up the subject with General Aaron of a future assignment to the DAO in Moscow.

"I haven't yet received a follow-on assignment from here, sir. Any chance I can get into the attaché pipeline?"

"You've been going to school all your life, haven't you?" General Aaron grinned.

"I guess it looks that way, sir. Either studying or teaching. But I did have a tour in Vietnam, that ASA tour in Berlin when I was enlisted, and an analytic job at the Pentagon. And I'm due for promotion soon."

"But your Russian experience has been only a series of desk jobs. I think you need to get your feet wet before you jump into the Soviet scene. You need to 'get your steel tempered.'" The general was referring to a 1935 Soviet classic, *Kak zakalyalas stal'* (How the Steel was Tempered), by N.A. Ostrovsky.

"How do I do that, sir?"

"I think you should spend a year in Heidelberg to get a feel for the strategic and operational situation in Europe, then spend some time with the Mission."

"What's the Mission?" I'd forgotten about the "missionaries" during the RB-66 shoot-down in 1964.

"There, you see? You're still a little wet behind the ears when it comes to real intelligence work in Europe."

My face flushed. He was right. What the heck was the Mission?

General Aaron said, "But don't you worry. Not only will you get to Moscow, but we're grooming you to become the Defense Attaché there some day."

It was clear to me I had a lot to learn. First of all, I needed to find out what the Mission was.

From Fort Huachuca I found myself assigned to the intelligence staff at Headquarters, U.S. Army, Europe (USAREUR) in Heidelberg. After a few weeks working in rotating shifts on the 24-hour Watch Team— continually monitoring the Soviet military situation in Eastern Europe—I was put in charge of the Daily Intelligence Cable. USAREUR sent this report to senior and subordinate units.

It was here I began to see the intelligence reports coming out of the Mission. At first, it was hard to believe we had people on the ground inside East Germany routinely observing Soviet and East German military activities. The Soviet reference to "missionaries" during the RB-66 shoot-down now came back to me.

USMLM reports were telling me an interesting story. For example, in September 1975, a USMLM Ground Team photographed a training poster indicating East German border guards were now being taught to fire on border violators from moving APCs, instead of their earlier practice of shooting only from fixed positions. In October, a USMLM Air Team photographed deployed electronic countermeasures equipment that until then had been seen only in the travel mode under tarp. That same month, a Ground Team photographed the deployment of an anti-aircraft element with all the troops in full chemical-biological-radiological gear. In December, an Air Team took close-up photography of an electronically modified Soviet helicopter. I looked at the picture and wondered: How did they get so close to the helicopter?

In February 1976, a USMLM Ground Team came upon a 207-vehicle column belonging to an artillery regiment. The team passed the column twice, counting the vehicles and writing down all the registration numbers from the vehicles' bumpers for later identification. In March, another Ground Team discovered and photographed for the first time a new Soviet ground surveillance radar. Air Teams were frequently photographing Soviet military aircraft that displayed new weapons or electronic gear. In June, a Ground Team confirmed the existence and location of a KGB signals regiment by picking up several documents and technical manuals from a trash dump just outside the Soviet installation fence.

I saw one detention report that partially answered my question about how the Mission teams got so close to their targets:

> Suhl. East Germany. On 27 July, a USMLM tour was detained while conducting reconnaissance of a communications site in Suhl. As the installation had appeared deserted, the USMLM tour officer felt it a justified risk to climb over two fences into the installation, where he was surprised and apprehended, camera in hand, by an armed East German sentry. The tour officer succeeded in removing and obliterating his film before the guard confiscated the camera at

gunpoint. Several Vopos were called to the scene,
together with the Soviet kommandant of Suhl, to
whom the USMLM officer surrendered his documents.
An Akt [official statement-jrh] was prepared, which
the tour officer refused to sign. Fourteen hours after
the initial detention, the tour was escorted back to
the main road and released. (1975 USMLM Unit
History)

All the reports provided small pieces to a larger
jigsaw-type picture of the capabilities and status of the
Soviet and East German armies and air forces. Much
of the technical information provided by USMLM to
our headquarters required further analysis by technical
experts in Heidelberg or Washington, DC. What was
of more immediate importance for us, however, was the
up-to-date reporting from the Mission on the activity
and combat status of the twenty Soviet motorized rifle
and tank divisions, as well as an artillery division and
an air army lined up behind the German segment of the
Iron Curtain.

All three Allied Military Liaison Missions became
heavily involved in the collection of information during
the semiannual Soviet troop rotations. Soviet soldiers
were almost all draftees, or conscripts, who served for two
years. This short period of active duty, which necessitated
frequent new replacements, caused considerable turbulence
in Soviet units. Every six months, a quarter of the soldiers
would be released from active duty and replaced in their
units by what we would call "raw recruits" (despite the
fact that, as I just indicated, they weren't recruits, but
rather draftees).

The impact of this rotation turbulence became a subject of special interest at HQ, USAREUR. The Deputy Chief of Staff for Intelligence, Major General Oliver Dillard, tasked me to prepare a research paper/staff study to determine what significance troop rotation had on GSFG combat effectiveness. I spent several weeks poring over historical documents from all available intelligence and open sources. One of the best sources for my study was a report from the Allied missions of a GSFG alert in 1973 called just outside Berlin by the newly arrived CINC, General Evgenii Ivanovsky. I concluded that the reported chaos created by this alert was such that the new CINC probably decided something had to be done differently. Since no such "Chinese fire drills" had been observed later in General Ivanovsky's tenure as CINC, my findings suggested the Soviets overcame the degradation in combat effectiveness by varying the number of conscripts assigned to each unit. Some units might be more degraded during one cycle; but, once trained up, they would be able to maintain their combat effectiveness during the time new conscripts were being placed in other units.

After a few months at USAREUR, I gained an appreciation for what the Mission did and greatly anticipated my assignment to Potsdam and Berlin. I had no official word, however, on whether I would in fact be assigned there from Heidelberg.

In the spring of 1976, the Chief of USMLM, Colonel Peter Thorsen, came to Heidelberg. During his visit, he asked to see me. I could tell this was going to be a job interview.

"So Captain Holbrook," he began, "General Aaron thinks you should become one of us in Potsdam."

"I'm really looking forward to it, sir."

"Tell me about yourself. I haven't reviewed your file yet."

I gave a short summary of my education and military experience up to my assignment at USAREUR.

"*I vy govorite po-russki khorosho*? You speak Russian well?"

"*Da*," I answered with a smile. "I've been working pretty hard on it for several years."

"You may not get that many chances to speak Russian at the Mission. We often work in silence, if you know what I mean. But when you need the Russian, you really need it."

"I also speak some German now, sir."

"Well, we usually leave that up to the tour NCOs, but it never hurts to know both languages. In any case, I'll get back to you on when, or whether, you'll be joining us."

By the end of my first year in Heidelberg, I was ordered to report to USMLM in Berlin.

PART III: TOURING IN EAST GERMANY

CHAPTER 10
HIER WIRD GESCHOSSEN!
(YOU WILL BE SHOT HERE!)

Late August, 1976. Three o'clock in the morning. The major and his driver picked me up at my quarters in the American Düppel Housing Area. Both were experienced tour personnel and were taking me on my first foray into East Germany on an intelligence collection mission. The major wanted an early start so we could be on target by daybreak. As we rode down Potsdamer Chaussee toward the border, I sat quietly and listened to the two men in the front seat discuss the first target. I was excited to be going on my first tour, but I felt a little awkward about being a third thumb, so to speak, and not yet a real tour officer.

Our entry point into East Germany was the Glienicke Bridge—the famous bridge where Gary Powers had been exchanged for Colonel Rudolph Abel in 1962. The Glienicke Bridge, also nicknamed "Freedom Bridge," had seen countless other quiet exchanges of spies and recovered remains of soldiers between the Soviets and Allies over the years. The bridge crossed the Havel River and marked the boundary between West Berlin and Potsdam. No regular traffic was allowed. Soviet guards manned a station in the middle of the bridge where we stopped our Opel Admiral and showed our Soviet passes before proceeding past the East German guards, whom we ignored.

"Watch for narks along the street or in an alley," said the major. "They'll probably be in a Wartburg or the old Buick." "Narks" was a term we used to refer to our East German surveillants.

Sure enough, we noticed the 1970 Buick, with two sleeping occupants, parked along the desolate street that led from the bridge. It was one of the few high-powered vehicles the *Stasi* used for surveilling Mission tours. *Stasi* was the German nickname for the MfS, the East German Security Service. *Stasi* became a commonly known word the world over after the fall of the Berlin Wall (1989) and later revelations about MfS activities during the Communist period in East Germany.

When we passed by the Buick, there was no reaction inside the MfS car. But we knew surveillants could pick us up at many junctures, not the least of which was when we departed the Potsdam House, where we were headed at the moment. An East German guard shack stood just outside our compound, and the occupant would surely notify the MfS that an American military tour was about to launch. Mission tours almost always stopped at the Potsdam House for their *Kiste*—a box full of enough sandwiches and coffee to sustain us for two to three days. We usually brought along some instant soup and, perhaps, some candy bars either to eat ourselves or to give to East German children along the way.

As we left the Potsdam House, a two-man surveillance team in an East German Wartburg began to follow.

"Wait until we reach the Autobahn," the major instructed his driver. "It'll be a simple matter losing them in the dark."

"Yeah," replied the driver, "It's not like they have a BMW or Mercedes."

In about fifteen minutes we reached the open road.

"O.K. Leave them in the dust," the major signaled to the driver.

We quickly reached 80 miles an hour and were gradually widening the gap between the narks and us. No one else was on the Autobahn. The major didn't need to say any more. In a few minutes, the driver flipped a toggle switch.

"We no longer have tail or brake lights," the major explained to me.

The distance between our car and the surveillants stretched to the point where I soon lost sight of them. The major pulled out a map from his folder and studied it by flashlight for a few moments.

"About two kilometers ahead is a dirt road that will take us into a forest where we can watch the narks go by. Then we'll sit for awhile before we continue on."

In about a minute the driver slowed our car down to 20 miles an hour and spun the steering wheel to the left. Almost instantly we were in the middle of a dark forest. We turned the vehicle around and waited. In five minutes, the MfS Wartburg went sailing by. After waiting another 15 minutes, we eased out onto the Autobahn again and proceeded to the target area—a Soviet installation we were planning to photograph that morning.

"They'll have given up on us by now," the major said as he turned to me. "It's not like this hasn't happened to them before. With one underpowered car, they don't stand a chance against us."

After a couple more hours of driving, we turned off the main road again to drive down a tank trail that ran a few hundred yards past the installation. Soon our car left the tank trail and we threaded the trees to approach closer to our target. I felt my muscles tense as the installation came into sight in the early dawn light. It was still about a hundred yards away, but I could see guard towers on the corners of the walls. I looked around and my eye caught a homemade sign nailed to a tree we had just passed, with the ominous message: "*Hier wird geschossen!*" Underneath the German were two words in Russian: "*Zdes' strelyayut!*" Both messages, translated into English, meant the same thing: 'You will be shot here!'

"Did you see that sign?" I whispered to both the men in the front seat. The major understood Russian and the driver understood German, so I knew they could read the messages if they saw them.

"Yeah, we see them all over the country," the major answered as he looked over at the driver. Both were now smiling. The major turned to me in the back seat.

"You have to get used to such attempts to scare us off. Besides, it's meant for Germans who might be strolling through the woods on a Sunday afternoon."

"You don't take the sign seriously then?"

"Yes and no. If we backed off every time we saw a warning sign, we'd never get anything done. Don't worry. We're going to get just close enough to check out the activity inside the installation and see if there's any new equipment there. As soon as we have enough light, we'll take some pictures."

"Fine," I said. "Just checking to see if you'd noticed."

An incident a little over a week earlier was still fresh in my mind. On 11 August, a Mission tour near Nedlitz stopped on a main road at a railroad crossing because the barrier was down. Several soldiers and an officer ran toward the vehicle in what appeared to be an attempt to detain the team. The USMLM tour quickly turned the car around and sped away from the barrier. As they did, the Soviets shouted and fired two shots at the vehicle. Fortunately, the vehicle was not hit. But I couldn't get the incident out of my mind. That tour had been in an open area and still got fired on. What could *we* expect, being this close to a Soviet installation?

I assumed a macho attitude and pretended the major's explanation was sufficient. After all, he was the experienced tour officer and I was along only as a "back-seater." Still, the earlier shooting incident kept me on edge.

After having been an analyst at the Pentagon and Headquarters, USAREUR, and a passive SIGINT collector at the 78th SOU in 1963-64, I was now going to become an active intelligence collector on the ground and in the middle of twenty-one Soviet divisions and an air army. I thought about the Mission reports I had read when I was in Heidelberg. Now I was going to see things first-hand and participate in writing those reports. This was the real thing—"where the rubber meets the road."

We had gone over the trip's targets together in Berlin for two days before setting out. The major and the driver had packed the car—a specially modified Opel Admiral—the night before. Modifications included a

35-gallon gas tank, allowing us to travel several hundred miles over a period of days without having to come out into the open to stop at an East German gas station. During some tours, we chose to travel off-road and in wooded areas where we hoped to avoid any exposure to the Soviet and East German military. For this off-road travel our cars were equipped with special suspension and extra plating under the chassis to protect the engine and transmission from tree stumps and rocks. This Opel had also been converted to four-wheel drive. The dashboard on all our touring vehicles showed an array of buttons and toggle switches we used to control the horn, as well as the front, rear, and interior lights for traveling dark or deceiving any onlookers or surveillance teams.

In the trunk we carried an axe, a shovel, a heavy-duty winch and 50 feet of steel cable, two nylon tow straps, a steel tow cable, and a tow chain. Included in our array of equipment was a "deadman"—a large steel plate that we could secure to the ground with a stake, if there were no trees nearby, and then hook our winch to it. The trunk also contained two four-foot "cheater boards" to place under the rear wheels to free the differential or to place across narrow ditches. And, of course, a box full of tools.

Beside me on the back seat was our intelligence collection equipment, packed in two large suitcase-type black bags. One held maps of various scales. Our "clobber" map—all of East Germany with an overlay of the Permanent Restricted Areas (PRA)—was the only map we showed Soviets in the event we were clobbered. The second bag contained extensive photo equipment, a tape recorder, and binoculars. Curtains covered our rear and two backseat windows, and we placed army blankets over the bags on the back seat. The only thing a passerby could see inside the car that might raise eyebrows would be the panel of buttons and toggle switches on the dashboard.

The driver slowed the vehicle. The major prepared two cameras, attaching on one an 85mm and on the other a 135mm lens. The sun was rising behind us. The major handed me the first camera.

"Take a panoramic of the entire installation in case we miss something we can pick up later when the film is developed," he told me.

"Gotcha."

The car stopped and the major slowly got out of the car. No light came on inside. He left the door ajar as he walked toward the installation. I began immediately to take pictures from left to right of the Soviet installation. I wanted to get out of the car also, so I could see beyond some larger trees that were blocking part of my view, but the major instructed me to stay in the car no matter what. He went to the edge of the tree line. I could see him taking pictures. Neither of us was using the automatic film advance motors on our cameras because they made too much noise. When I finished my photographing, I watched the major. I held my breath as he slung his camera over his shoulder and moved up to a high piece of ground. From there he took a few more pictures looking down into the installation. Then he returned to the car.

"Didn't see anything particularly interesting," he said. "But you never know. We'll see what we have when we get back to Berlin."

The driver performed the complicated maneuver of turning the car around among the trees, and we slowly departed the area. At no time did we get any reaction from the Soviet soldiers who were supposed to be guarding the installation. As we rode out of the forest back to the tank trail we had driven in on, the major and I rewound our films and logged them in on a note pad. The major handed his film back to me and I placed all the rolls in my field jacket pocket. Exposed film would always remain on our persons.

"There," he said turning to me, "that's how it's done. Any questions?"

"What if someone had seen you and started shooting?"

"I'd have run like hell for the car," he laughed.

"But the car's not bulletproof."

"No, that's true. But they don't often shoot at us. And when they do, they usually shoot in the air."

Our first target completed. I realized that the major telling me to photograph the installation from the car might have had another purpose besides getting a backup panorama. He knew very well that when we compared the shots on both films back in Berlin, it would become obvious to me how much better the "take" on this installation was on his film. To get really good coverage, I thought, I'm going to have to be aggressive and take some chances. It was clear to me that what counted, within reason, was not what we did or how we did it, but what we came home with.

CHAPTER 11
SIE HABEN EINEN NEUEN PRÄSIDENTEN
(YOU HAVE A NEW PRESIDENT)

"I don't know what's wrong, sir," my driver said, as we began to lurch and jerk along a minor road west of Eisleben. We pulled over to the side. The driver killed the engine, got out, and lifted the hood of our Bronco. After wiggling some wires around, removing and wiping off the distributor cap, he got back in and pressed the starter. Nothing.

"It was working alright when I checked it out back in Berlin," said the driver.

"Well, our vehicles do take a real beating. They're bound to break down from time to time," I said, partly to reassure the driver I didn't blame him for this development. Our touring vehicles rarely were allowed to run much over 25,000 miles before they had to undergo major service.

"What'll we do now?" asked the driver.

"I guess we just wait for it to cool down and try to start it again. If that doesn't work, we'll have to flag someone down and one of us will have to get a ride to

Blankenheim. Where's surveillance when you need it?" I said with a laugh.

In a few minutes, a Soviet UAZ-469 jeep came down the road. I got out, blocked the rear license plate with my body, and watched it approach. Without a signal from me, the UAZ slowed down and pulled over. The driver, a *praporschik*, a Soviet warrant officer, was alone.

"What's the matter? Car trouble?" he asked in Russian.

"Yes, we were having some trouble along the way and now it just won't start," I replied.

"Let me take a look at it," he said as he began to realize he had encountered two soldiers who weren't Soviets.

"We'd be much obliged."

"Who are you?" he asked, when he saw the front license plate.

"We're members of the U.S. Military Liaison Mission to your headquarters in Zossen-Wünsdorf. Army-General Ivanovsky's headquarters." I pretended he hadn't noticed the license plate that read, in Russian, exactly what I had just told him.

The *praporschik* hesitated a moment, but then seemed to be satisfied we must have some approved, official status in East Germany. He looked under the hood and examined the engine. In about five minutes, he told my driver, who had been watching him work, to try to start the vehicle again. This time it started.

"What'd he do?" I asked my driver.

"I'm not sure. He must have found a loose wire I missed."

"*Bol'shoe spasibo*, thank you very much," I told the Soviet. "Would you like a pack of American cigarettes?

What's your name? We'll put in a good word for you at your headquarters."

He looked at the cigarettes and me for a moment, then replied, "*Nichevo*, it was nothing. I don't smoke. You don't need to say anything in Wünsdorf." He quickly got back in his vehicle and pulled away.

We continued our journey towards Nordhausen. We were going to check some military facilities in the Harz, a mountain range that straddles the central part of the Intra-German border. Along the way, in the lower elevations, we were hoping to see whatever fall foliage remained. It was 2 November, as we were to be reminded later.

When we returned from the Harz later, we pulled into a forest. After a night there, we awoke about 4 a.m. and prepared to renew our collection effort before heading back to Potsdam and Berlin. We left our overnight spot and headed toward our target. It was still too dark to see anything when we arrived in the area, so we stopped near a small settlement of three houses and a grove of large trees. The driver parked the car, keeping the trees between us and the nearest house. The sky was clear; there was no moon, but the stars provided some light. We got out of the car to stretch our legs and have a smoke. While we were admiring the sky and the stillness, a stranger's voice startled us.

"*Sie haben einen neuen Präsidenten*" (You have a new president.)

I looked around, but could see no one.

"Does that mean Carter won the election?" I asked in German as I moved toward the trees.

"*Ja*."

Yesterday had been Election Day. My driver and I had voted by absentee ballot back in Berlin before we departed two days earlier. It was now close to 5 a.m. local time, which meant it was almost 11 p.m. the night before on the U.S. east coast.

"How did you find out?"

"I listen to BBC."

On the other side of a large tree I could make out the profile of someone. His voice sounded to me as though it belonged to an older man. He was smoking a pipe, which I could now smell. I stopped at the near edge of the tree.

"That's good to hear," I said. "We appreciate your giving us the news. This is the first we heard of it."

"I saw the license plate on your vehicle. I know you're Americans, but I don't know why you're here."

When we drove up we had our headlights off and must not have seen him somewhere on our side of the trees.

"Yes. We're American liaison officers to the Soviet Army. We've been traveling around the GDR and decided to stop for a rest."

"Welcome. It's good to see Americans again."

"When's the last time you saw an American?"

"In 1945. I was a prisoner of war in Arizona from 1943 to the end of the war. It was a very nice time."

"I'm glad you were treated well," I said. Former German POWs who had spent time during WWII in the States had approached me before in various towns. Without exception, they were all smiles and "happy to see Americans again." I thought of their experiences compared to those of U.S. POWs in German prison camps.

"Too bad we had to be occupied by the Red Army instead of the American Army," my interlocutor said. I would hear that lament again a few times before I left East Germany.

He began to walk around the trees. I moved toward him. When we met, we shook hands. Up close, I could see he was in his 60s. He wore farmer's overalls and a cap. I changed the topic.

"I see you're smoking a pipe. Would you like some American tobacco?"

A few moments of silence. Then, "*Ja*, that would be nice."

He pulled out a small pouch from his back pocket into which I emptied some tobacco. He held it up to his nose and smelled the tobacco.

"Very nice aroma," he said.

"Thank you. People say it smells somewhat like vanilla."

He shook my hand again, this time more firmly. "Thank you very much. I wish the best to you and your new president," he said as he turned and walked back to his house. I returned to the Bronco, where my sergeant and I remained a little longer before resuming our tour.

Later that day we were back in the Harz. Whatever the Soviet warrant officer had done to repair our engine either came undone or something else went wrong. The engine died again just before noon. Fortunately, we were on top of a mountain. We pushed the Bronco to a point where we could get in and coast down the hill. About five miles down the road, we came to a small village and pulled into the parking lot of a *Gaststätte*—a German pub.

"This looks like as good a place as any to stop," I said. "We can call for a recovery team from Berlin."

Whenever we needed to communicate with home base, we called the Potsdam House from a civilian telephone. It was not the easiest thing to do from the antiquated East German telephone system, but we had no choice. We had no phones or radios in our vehicles, although USMLM touring vehicles had them in the mid-60s. The USMLM unit histories for 1966 and 1967 report the radios were standard commercial sets with a 50-mile range, considered "sufficient to allow a tour to report significant indicators without having to cross into West Berlin or rely on East German commercial communications." Although one would think the radios were considered, as the histories state: "a significant improvement in USMLM's capability to perform effectively in critical situations where the Soviets would certainly attempt to interfere or prevent reporting," that turned out not to be the case.

I recently talked to a former tour officer who had been at USMLM during 1966-67. It turns out the radios weren't such a good idea. There were many reasons for this. First, the Soviets would be able to intercept any transmission and possibly fix the location of the sender. Second, the antennas necessary for the radios to work effectively were very prominent, diminishing the "innocent cover" of USMLM vehicles. Long whip-type antennas on Mission cars would make the vehicles look more offensive to the Soviets and East Germans. Using antennas that could be erected after the car stopped wasn't a good idea either. According to another former tour officer, to erect the antenna wire "would require someone climbing a pretty tall tree to string it." Finally, higher headquarters in the Western Zone or even Washington, DC, could interfere with the collection tasks the Mission teams were pursuing. There certainly had been enough of that type of micro-management (usually from senior officers flying in helicopters) in Vietnam.

Although, at first glance, radios would facilitate reporting on indicators of the Imminence of Hostilities (IOH), most Missionaries agreed that the best, and perhaps only, IOH indicator of all would have been that a USMLM tour would not be permitted into East Germany in the first place. Or tours that were already out would never return.

I found a phone in the *Gaststätte* and called the Potsdam House to ask for the recovery team. The Potsdam OIC, Lieutenant Berner, told me it would take about ten hours for the team to reach us. We made sure we had our film and notes in our pockets and that everything was out of sight in the car before we locked it and went back inside to have a nice schnitzel dinner and a couple of beers.

The Germans, of course, took great interest in their visitors from the West. We began to chat with them in German, answering their questions about America and asking them about their lives. They were friendly and happy to talk with Americans. It wasn't the first time they had met foreign Military Liaison Mission members. In the past, there had been other Mission teams who stopped by this small *Gaststätte* for a meal. They too had heard the results of the U.S. presidential election and asked us what kind of a person this Jimmy Carter was. I was a little embarrassed to say I didn't really know. All I could say was that he was a Naval Academy graduate and had been the governor of the state of Georgia.

Throughout my time with the Mission, I didn't have many chances to sit around and talk with East Germans. We rarely went to restaurants or bars or even walked around the streets of Potsdam. The Germans we met in hotels during our travels around the GDR, on those rare occasions when we overnighted in hotels, were trained to deal with foreign tourists. Almost all our time in the GDR was business. For the most part, Mission teams worked on collecting intelligence information, so we often tried to avoid contact with civilians. Once in awhile, we would take our families on what we called "cultural tours" to cities like Leipzig, Dresden, or Wittenberg-Lutherstadt for sight-seeing.

Photo 15: One of many signs we saw as we traveled about the GDR. This one reads, "*Druzhba* (the Russian word for friendship) is called *Freundschaft*" (the German word for friendship). Real friendship between the Germans and Soviets, however, was seldom observed by USMLM.

The Germans in the *Gaststätte* already knew we were attached to the Soviet Army headquarters. They apparently had an idea what we did during our travels and avoided asking any inappropriate questions. They didn't hesitate, however, to talk about the disadvantages they had to live with because they were occupied by the Soviets and had to put up with the SED—the East German ruling, essentially, Communist Party. The issue of the American withdrawal from the region at the end of World War II came up again.

Incidentally, I noticed these Germans didn't like their beer cold. When it came out of the tap, they'd walk over to the end of the counter, take an electric coil like one we use to heat coffee, put it in their beer for a few seconds, and then return happily to their tables. I tried it also and found it to be a good idea. German beer has a nice aroma that diminishes when the beer is chilled.

In the evening we ate another meal; this time I had sauerbraten (roast pork), and we drank another couple of beers. The sauerbraten had a special meaning for me. A few years earlier, I'd met Niño Cochise in Willcox, Arizona. He was the grandson of the great Apache Chief and had served nearly forty years off and on in the U.S. Air Force. He'd flown in the Berlin Airlift and was 101 years old at the time I met him. When he learned I was on my way to Germany, the first thing he did was ask me: *"Sprechen Sie Deutsch?"* (Do you speak German?) Then he recommended I try sauerbraten, as it was his favorite German dish.

Our recovery team arrived after dark. By then my driver, the Germans, and I were all in a jovial mood. It was one of the few nice breaks from the normal tense collection atmosphere we usually experienced during service in East Germany.

CHAPTER 12
WATCH FOR SIGNS THE SOVIETS MIGHT ATTACK

Many remember the Cold War as a time of fear and tension. The awesome arsenals of thermonuclear weapons both the Soviet Union and the United States possessed created an atmosphere of potentially impending doom to civilizations the world over. At times, especially during the 1950s, civil defense protection against a nuclear attack occupied the minds and resources of many public institutions and individuals, both here and in the Soviet Union. The 1962 Cuban Missile Crisis seemed to be a reminder of the calamity that could befall mankind.

As the Cold War droned on, however, there were other, less catastrophic, military operations by the USSR and the U.S. that seemed to be permitted by these two superpowers as being below the threshold of thermonuclear exchange. The Soviet invasions of Hungary in 1956, of Czechoslovakia in 1968, of Afghanistan in 1979, and the American war in Vietnam are the most prominent examples.

Among the tasks USMLM was in a unique place to carry out was the detection on the ground, close up and personal, of Soviet and East German military activities that might presage an attack on NATO. This task involved a search by USMLM and the other two Allied Military Liaison Missions for indicators that might point to what we called the Imminence of Hostilities (IOH). Other intelligence organizations also watched for IOH signs, but the Missions were doing it "behind enemy lines," in the midst of the largest concentration of Soviet forces in the world.

Retired Colonel Paul Skowronek, Chief, USMLM, from 1964 to 1966, wrote in his PhD dissertation that "there were no warnings to alert the West to mobilization preparations" for the Soviet invasions of Hungary in 1956 and Czechoslovakia in 1968. He is probably wrong on the 1956 invasion, and certainly wrong about 1968. In fairness to Skowronek, no 1956 USMLM Unit History exists and the 1968 Unit History was not yet available for his research. In fact, the latter was declassified only in 2006.

In the early morning hours on 20 August 1968, Warsaw Pact armies, led of course by the Soviets, invaded Czechoslovakia. I was in our unit officers' club in Vietnam when I got the news. At the time, I was commanding an intelligence detachment with an infantry brigade. Soviet military affairs had temporarily taken a backseat to my focus on the Viet Cong and the North Vietnamese army. I was vaguely aware of the political turmoil in Czechoslovakia, associated with Alexander Dubcek's reforms—which came to be known as the Prague Spring—from the *Stars and Stripes* newspaper and Armed Forces radio. But I was surprised the Soviets had actually invaded a brother socialist country. It had been twelve years since the Hungarian invasion and I thought that during 'modern times,' that kind of dangerous military action by the Soviets in Europe was a thing of the past. A lesson learned: the Soviets were apt to do whatever they wanted, regardless of the futility of their actions or the repercussions in the international community. I immediately bought a drink for everyone at my table and proposed a toast to the Czechoslovak people.

The invasion came as no surprise, however, to the men and women at USMLM and the other Allied Missions. As summarized in the 1968 Unit History, the Missions had reported that:

> A major portion of GSFG and East Germany units were involved in a series of military operations that culminated in the occupation of Czechoslovakia. Additionally, there were important movements of non-GSFG units through the Soviet Zone of Germany towards the Czech border. This crucial relocation of military forces was the priority target for USMLM operational activities during the period 10 May through 14 November.

Certain unexpected events began to occur, or anticipated events failed to materialize. USMLM reported that a Warsaw Pact exercise scheduled for spring in the southwest portion of East Germany was apparently canceled. Already in early May, the Mission reported that elements of two Soviet tank divisions had moved to the Czechoslovak border. A new restricted area was imposed on the Missions that essentially prevented observation of garrisons of two more tank divisions and two motorized rifle (infantry) divisions. On 1 June, the

Soviet headquarters created twelve new areas that were now permanently off limits to Mission observation. These areas included eleven Soviet airfields and five additional garrison towns. New restricted areas continued to appear throughout the pre-invasion months.

The Missions began to pay more attention to the military units outside the restricted areas. They discovered that some installations not considered significant by themselves could show telltale signs of their parent, larger combat units. For example, a "relatively minor ammunition storage facility" in Halle mirrored the activity of the 27th Guards Motorized Rifle Division. On 26 July, the facility contained its usual number and type of ammunition trailers. On 29 July, the facility was completely empty. By this date, the 27th division had also departed its garrison.

The Missions also patrolled the Autobahns in the southeast quadrant of East Germany almost around the clock. (USMLM was for a long time during the critical months at fifty percent strength for Army officers, as the Vietnam War was causing curtailment of tours in Europe.) The Missions continued to report large and small columns of military vehicles heading for Czechoslovakia along major routes adjacent to the Autobahns.

USMLM Air Teams reported redeployments from Soviet airfields around East Germany to those near the Czech border. They noted the aircraft apparently destined to participate in the invasion were marked with two red stripes on their fuselages. Air Teams also identified new configurations of weapons and electronic gear on aircraft and the use by the Soviets of makeshift grass airfields.

Equally important for NATO and the U.S. were reports from the Allied Military Missions of Warsaw Pact units leaving Czechoslovakia after the invasion. On 4 September, a USMLM Air Team reported a northbound column of 16 ambulances, 15 busses and a jeep. The busses carried bandaged troops on stretchers. On 27 October, USMLM reported that the city of Halle sported flags welcoming home the 27th Guards Motorized Rifle Division. On 12 November, Allied Missions coordinated efforts to cover the return of another Rifle division and a tank division. By the end of November, most Soviet troops were back at their usual routine in East Germany. USMLM and the Allied Missions had been on top of the situation before and after the invasion.

Curious as to why Colonel Skowronek would say there were no warnings of the impending invasion of Czechoslovakia, I interviewed retired Brigadier General Randall Greenwalt, who served as a tour officer at the Mission in 1968, was my Ground Team Chief in 1976-77, and later became Chief of USMLM in 1981.

General Greenwalt pointed out that the IOH indicators reported by the Mission in 1968 "were treated with great significance by the military commands within the European theater." In Washington, however, it was another matter. According to General Greenwalt, the IOH indicators reported by USMLM in 1968 may have been "trumped" by analysts and policymakers in Washington who were "focused on diplomatic and political developments, not pragmatic military IOH indicators." General Greenwalt doubted those who were following political developments between the Soviet Union and Prague were even aware of the USMLM IOH reports that were appearing in USAREUR's Daily Intelligence Summary at the time.

The failure in Washington to properly assess USMLM's reports in 1968 highlights a serious weakness that is by no means a thing of the past. Yes, Pearl Harbor in 1941 is a classic example, but similar failures were articulated also by the 9/11 report. Such failures can be corrected only if: 1) intelligence information reaches the right policymakers in time, 2) policymakers attach appropriate significance to the information reported to them, and 3) intelligence is not skewed to fit political motives at the top of our government.

Regarding the invasion of Czechoslovakia, General Greenwalt echoed the advice of many intelligence professionals who warn of the inherent dangers in the predispositions of national policymakers to let their strategic assumptions outweigh countervailing, low-level, purely military indicators. Doubts apparently existed also in British circles during Soviet preparations for the invasion of Czechoslovakia. Geraghty quotes one former BRIXMIS officer who remarked, "'We said they are going to fight.' Higher Command said, 'But you don't invade another country in Europe in the 1960s.'" Higher Command was wrong, as was I in Vietnam when I was surprised by the Soviet invasion.

I'm convinced that USMLM and the other Allied Missions running all over the East German countryside, watching the Soviets as they moved around and trained, contributed significantly to our knowledge of possible Soviet preparations for war. I mentioned in the previous chapter that there were measures the Soviets would probably take to neutralize the Mission teams in the event they were planning a military attack against the West—not permit Mission tours into East Germany at all, or capture all the tours that were already out. Still, preparations for a ground war take a lot of time and it's doubtful the Soviets could have hidden preparations for such an attack from all the Missions. The 1968 Soviet invasion of Czechoslovakia was a case in point.

During my service with USMLM, no events comparable to the invasions of Hungary or Czechoslovakia took place. In fact, verifying that suspicious activity was not a cause for concern was also important. Once, the USMLM Operations Officer sent a driver and me to the Intra-German border area west of Magdeburg to check out a report that hundreds of trucks were lined up on the East German side. When we arrived, we found the trucks were all commercial 18-wheelers, waiting for entry permission into West Germany. The drivers told me there had been a strike somewhere in West Germany and the truckers were stranded on the East German side of the border until everything was resolved.

It is true the Missions' IOH role gradually became less critical as new, sophisticated strategic surveillance systems became available. Nonetheless, the Military Liaison Missions' ability to report significant changes on the ground, in the midst of such a large concentration of the Soviet Army's best men and equipment, remained an important trip wire in the event the Soviets were preparing for an attack on a NATO country.

CHAPTER 13
LOCK AND LOAD

19 November 1976. The infamous Satzkorn bridge, site of frequent detentions in Tri-Mission history, maintained its notoriety with a potentially serious detention of a USMLM tour. As the tour vehicle proceeded across the bridge, a red rope/wire was pulled taut across the roadway in front of the car. Ten armed Soviet soldiers immediately blocked and surrounded the vehicle. Soviet AKMs [assault rifles-jrh] were trained on the tour and at least one soldier chambered a round. The lieutenant in charge was rude and aggressive. The tour was escorted to the Dallgow/Elster kommandatura and later to the Potsdam kommandatura where, after the usual charges, the tour was released. No Akt was prepared. It was subsequently determined that elements of the 35 MRD [motorized rifle division-jrh] were on-loading at Satzkorn at the time of the detention. However, once again our "right" to unimpeded travel was challenged and the safety of the tour jeopardized by the use of the cable and the unnecessary brandishing of loaded weapons. (USMLM Unit History, 1976)

A few weeks after the presidential elections, Staff Sergeant Germaine and I were returning to West Berlin from Leipzig in the middle of the morning. The night before, at our hotel, we'd encountered an unusually suspicious person in civilian clothes. He called himself Klaus and spoke both Russian and German like a native. (He may have been a Volga German from the USSR.) We sat around a table and talked about America, Germany, and the Soviet Union, although I had to keep fending off political and intelligence-related questions. He asked whether Sergeant Germaine understood German. Having established that to be so, Klaus switched to Russian when he touched upon intelligence questions. He kept pressing me to take a message to our intelligence people in Berlin. He said he had important information and wanted to make contact with our people. Ralph and I both concluded it was a transparent provocation. This Klaus would never have approached us in public like that, knowing we were under surveillance by MfS agents. So we assured him we had nothing to do with intelligence. (It was one of the few encounters I had in East Germany when someone obviously tried to elicit intelligence information from me. I reported it when I got back to Berlin, to both my own unit and to Berlin counterintelligence.)

About 1 a.m., after drinking and eating all evening, we excused ourselves and returned to our room. Klaus, our German or Russian "friend," apparently went to his room and must have assumed we would be going to sleep. If there were other surveillants in the hotel—and I'm sure there were—they must have come to the same conclusion. We waited an hour and then left the hotel through the rear exit, drove to a lucrative target without any surveillance and returned before daybreak. (More details on this target are in Chapter 17.)

The next day, in celebration of our success, I was smoking a cigar as we motored through Potsdam on our way back to Berlin. We were both feeling great. Before we left Berlin, Sergeant Germaine was informed he'd been selected to present a Mission gift to the U.S. Army Chief of Staff, General Bernard Rogers, who was visiting the Mission that day. Naturally, we were anxious to get back.

As we started across a bridge on the highway, a chain snapped up in front of us. Sergeant Germaine slammed on the Opel's brakes and we screeched into the chain barrier. From underneath the bridge a squad of armed Soviet soldiers scrambled up onto the bridge and pointed their rifles at us. They were led by a lieutenant.

"What the hell!" Sergeant Germaine said as he looked over at me.

"I don't know what this is," I said.

Having rifles pointed at one is not a comfortable feeling. This had never happened before to either of us in East Germany. Once, on an earlier tour in East Germany, as we came around a corner in the middle of a forest, a solitary, armed Soviet soldier guarding his installation had confronted my driver and me. He was as surprised by us as we were to see him. He didn't point his rifle at us, however, and I was able to extricate us from that situation by not speaking Russian at all, but rather making hand signals to the effect that we were lost and would immediately back away.

The lieutenant came over to my side of the Opel. I rolled down the window.

"What the hell is this all about," I shouted at him. He asked me for my pass.

"Why should I give my pass to some young lieutenant who doesn't have enough sense to have his soldiers lower their weapons. What if one of them gets the crazy idea to be a hero and shoot an American soldier." I didn't sound frightened, but I was.

The lieutenant turned back to his soldiers and gave some kind of signal. They all drew back the mechanisms on their AK-47 assault rifles, presumably putting a round into the firing chamber. I was concerned one of the soldiers would make a mistake and bump his trigger. In retrospect, the weapons were probably not loaded, or the rounds were blanks, as the Soviets rationed their ammunition very carefully. Moreover, given the lack of trust in their own soldiers, the Soviets probably wouldn't have let a patrol run around with live ammo. But I've always felt even unloaded weapons are "loaded."

"Let me see your pass," he repeated.

Sergeant Germaine and I looked at each other. We were still somewhat in shock at having the rifles pointed at us. Being detained by a group of Soviet soldiers was historically the most dangerous of all clobbers. Not only were Soviet soldiers inclined to manhandle Mission personnel, but also they often ignored, or were ignorant of, a Mission vehicle's extraterritorial status. Only a couple of years earlier, in 1974, they had caught one tour officer and his driver outside their unlocked vehicle, entered it, and confiscated all the tour equipment. A couple of months later, Soviet soldiers forced another tour officer and his driver from their unlocked car and, once again, took their equipment. Despite my upbraiding of the lieutenant, I was grateful he was present and hoped he could keep control of the situation.

"What's he want, sir?"

"He wants my pass."

"I'd give it to him if I were you."

"Shit, Ralph," I said as I handed over my pass. "This is going to make us late getting back to the Mission for General Roger's visit."

"Let's not think about that right now."

The lieutenant took the pass and backed off toward his soldiers. One of them handed him a radio/telephone on which he made a call. In about half an hour, an UAZ jeep pulled up and out stepped a captain. They talked for a moment, then the captain put my pass in his pocket and came over to me.

"I'm going to escort you to the *komendatura*," he said.

"What's this all about?" I demanded. "What kind of a professional officer would allow those young conscripts to lock and load their weapons and point them at accredited American military representatives? How long has that lieutenant been in the Army? How long have *you* been in the Army? You know those soldiers are just kids. What if one of them does something foolish? And besides, we were just on our way back to Berlin from Leipzig. What right do you have to detain us here?"

"You speak very good Russian," he said as he smiled at me.

"So do you," I shot back.

"Of course. I'm a Russian." His smile disappeared. "Follow me." Without further words, he went back to his jeep and motioned us to fall in behind him.

I was angry. Primarily because this was a nonsensical detention that would interfere with my driver's chance to present the gift to General Rogers. (If the Soviet captain only knew that the gift Sergeant Germaine was to present was a Soviet Army belt!) Although I was concerned this detention would upset our own schedule back in Berlin, I had lost some of my fear of being detained. The Soviets had me in their grip once before and didn't do anything frightening. Besides, this clobber wouldn't have any impact on our mission, since we had already completed our work.

My anger had not fully subsided when at the *komendatura* I was put in a room with no table, but several chairs. (Ralph remained in the car, as drivers always did, to protect our equipment.) The captain left me alone, except for a private who had been assigned to guard me. Whether he was from the armed squad I don't know, but he too had an AK-47 slung over his shoulder. While waiting for an officer to appear, I realized I had to use the latrine. I told the private. He said I couldn't leave the room. A few minutes later, I told the private that I really had to go.

"You must stay here," he said. "I have my orders."

"Listen, soldier. If you don't let me go to the latrine or escort me to one right now, I'm going to piss in the corner over there."

The private looked at me as if he didn't believe what he was hearing. I meant every word of it. No one can fight Mother Nature. And I wasn't going to go in my trousers. Finally, he motioned for me to follow him and shortly thereafter I returned to the room, relieved, but still a little hot under the collar.

When the captain returned to the room, I demanded to know why we had been detained. I told him my Mission chief would lodge a formal complaint with HQ, GSFG. The captain gave me no answers, but simply told me to follow him. We walked down the corridor past several surprised and curious soldiers and officers, then entered what appeared to be a conference room with two officers seated at a table. Aha, I thought, this was going to be a little different than my last clobber. My concern about getting Sergeant Germaine back to the Mission in time for the general's visit began to be replaced by concern for what was going to happen to me.

"Mr. Holbrook," a major addressed me. "What were you doing near the Satzkorn railroad siding this morning at 6 a.m.?" Soviet officers always refused to address us by our rank.

"I don't know what you're talking about. We were nowhere near Potsdam this morning. We were returning from Leipzig when this young lieutenant unleashed a bunch of young soldiers with weapons on us. For no reason. Surely your surveillance can verify we were on the way from Leipzig this morning at that time."

"We have witnesses who saw a Military Liaison Mission car parked near the siding."

"That may be so. But it wasn't us."

The Soviet officers consulted among themselves. The captain got up and left the room. While he was gone, I verbally attacked the major again.

"Young man," I said. He was a lot younger than me, even though we were both majors. I refused to call him major. "Do you realize you're going to make us late for an important ceremony in Berlin with our army's

Chief of Staff? That's equivalent to your Commander in Chief, Soviet Ground Forces. My sergeant has been given the honor of presenting the general with a gift and if this drags on, we'll never make it back in time. I feel responsible for him, but it's really you who will bear the responsibility if we don't make the ceremony."

"Calm down, Mr. Holbrook. We'll sort this out."

Just then I heard a commotion in the corridor. Someone was shouting profanity and I could hear scuffling. Then I saw two soldiers drag a third past the doorway. The third soldier was apparently drunk and was swearing like only Soviet soldiers can. The Russian term for profanity is *mat*, and this soldier was swearing in what the Russians call "three-story *mat*." I saw one of the soldiers hit the drunken one in the head with the butt of a rifle. Just as quickly as the commotion had started, it ended and the soldiers were out of sight.

"What was that all about?" I interrupted my tirade against the major.

"None of your business," said the major as he got up and closed the door.

Soon the captain who had left the room returned. He leaned over to the major and whispered something. After a short exchange, the major turned to me and said I could go. No apology for my detention. No explanation why I was being released. But I noticed he never brought up the question of my signing an *Akt*. Akts were protocol documents that summarized the situation and the reason for detentions. Officers at USMLM and, presumably, officers at the other Allied Missions, always refused to sign them or any other document. The Soviets knew this, but they persisted in asking us to sign these documents anyway.

The Soviets gave me my pass and I quickly returned to the car. We roared off toward Berlin, making it back in time for the ceremony. I later learned there had been a French Military Liaison tour in the Potsdam area that morning and apparently it was they who had been observing the Satzkorn railroad siding. We just happened to be at the wrong place at the wrong time.

Photo 16: Staff Sergeant Ralph Germaine presents Army Chief of Staff, General Bernard Rogers, with a Soviet army belt. Staff Sergeant Karl Mabardy, one of my drivers at USMLM, is standing immediately to Ralph's left.

One of the things I was learning was to be assertive with the Soviets. This tactic was reinforced in me when I watched my chief, Colonel Thorsen, deal with the Russians. He mixed assertiveness with conciliatory approaches to keep the Soviets off guard. I also thought about the infamous case in 1961, when the United States did not stand up to the Soviets and East Germans as they began to erect the Berlin Wall. Intelligence reports that subsequently became public showed the Communists were prepared to back down on that operation at the least sign of resistance from the Allies. Murphy, in an account of that event, wrote: "Barbed wire and posts... were first erected to test Western reactions... construction of the actual wall did not begin until after it was clear that no Western reaction was forthcoming." In other words, we had "let" them build the wall with no real opposition.

In my encounters with the Russians during my two clobbers so far, I found that by taking a hard line I got more respect from them. I have no doubt that had I not ranted and raved at them during this clobber, we may very well not have made it back to Berlin in time for the Chief of Staff's visit.

Chapter 14
Hallelujah, They've
Moved the Border!

Sergeant Jim Rice and I had come upon a Soviet training exercise east of Waltershausen, between the Ohrdruf and Gotha PRAs in southwest East Germany. Immediately we wondered whether a Temporary Restricted Area (TRA) had been declared since our departure from Potsdam two days earlier. If so, the Soviets could have used the TRA to link the two PRAs. It could also have blocked our only travel route in the area—Autobahn E63. No matter, we were here and we intended to exploit any opportunities that might arise.

From the number of soldiers and the types of vehicles, we concluded we had a motorized rifle (MR) battalion in our sights. It was November and that would be about right, I thought, for this stage of the GSFG training cycle. The presence of three tanks (that we could see) was not unusual for an MR battalion; the Soviets often attached tanks to MR units and infantry to tank units. An MR regiment had a whole battalion of tanks from which to draw reinforcements for a battalion.

We needed to get some vehicle registration numbers (VRN) in order to identify the unit. We stopped our Bronco and I began to photograph the entire scene while Jim kept a lookout for signs that someone would recognize who we were and attempt to detain us. When you're looking into the eyepiece of a camera, you miss a lot on the periphery. We kept our Bronco running, just in case. Our vehicle was painted olive drab and resembled the Soviet jeep-like UAZ-469. For the next few minutes no one paid any attention to us.

There didn't seem to be any new technology in the battalion. I leaned out my window with my camera and got side numbers from two of the tanks and a VRN from a communications van. The battalion was stopped and no vehicle movement was underway. They were pointed toward the Gotha PRA and may have been in reserve for another unit already in there.

"Here we go," Jim tapped me on the shoulder.

I pulled the camera into the car and looked around.

"There, on the left. A BTR-60 is turning toward us," Jim said.

The BTR-60 is an armored personnel carrier (APC) with eight-wheel drive. We were in for a ride. Jim needed no instructions from me. He spun our vehicle around in the snow and we took off. I fastened my seat belt. The BTR-60 sped up. It was cold enough that the snow wasn't too slippery so we had pretty good traction. We could go faster than the BTR-60, but we still had to be careful. We were on a side road about five miles from the Autobahn. The driver of the BTR-60 apparently was unconcerned about road conditions and began to gain on us.

"What'll he do if he does catch us?" Jim asked. "He can't block us in with only one vehicle."

"He probably has soldiers inside. They could surround us," I said.

"I'd hate to be one of them hanging on inside," he laughed.

In a few minutes we could see cars and trucks on the Autobahn, but we were still some distance away and it looked like we might not make it before the APC caught up to us.

"Let's cut across the field toward the Autobahn, if you think we can get through it," I said. "The BTR-60 will probably follow us, but we can get to the main highway much quicker."

Sergeant Rice turned right onto the frozen field. The BTR-60 did the same. Now I hoped we wouldn't run into any unseen ditches or other barriers along the way.

"I think this field is going to be alright," Jim said. We sped up some and were now keeping our distance from the BTR-60. In a couple of minutes we reached the edge of the Autobahn and churned up snow as we climbed the embankment to the highway surface.

"Which way, sir?"

"Make a right, we'll head for Eisenach."

The BTR-60 slowed as it approached the embankment. I watched in the rear view mirror and saw it come to a halt. On another occasion, a Soviet truck had chased us, but we found it easy to outmaneuver the truck in the woods. This APC, however, had given us a run for our money. We continued toward Eisenach until we came to a *Parkplatz* (a rest area) along the road. "Let's pull in and take a break," I said.

When we turned off into the *Parkplatz,* there were only two other vehicles there—both East German commercial trucks. The drivers were standing outside their vehicles talking and smoking. We parked a short distance away from them, made sure our gear was covered with Army blankets, and got out. Since our thermoses were empty, we set up our Coleman stove on the Bronco tailgate to heat water for coffee. The truck drivers looked over and one pointed at us. He was probably pointing to the license plate on the front of the Bronco with the American flag painted on it. In a few minutes they both walked over to us.

"Sind Sie Amerikaner? Are you Americans?" one asked.

"Ja," replied Jim. All our drivers spoke German and by now I spoke it also. So the conversation continued in German.

"Why are you here? Who are you?" asked the second truck driver.

"We're members of the U.S. Military Liaison Mission attached to the commander of the Soviet forces," Jim said.

"But you're a long way from the Soviet headquarters."

"Yes, we often travel around the GDR."

"Oh, I see," smiled one of the truck drivers. "You're spying on the Russians."

"No," I broke in. "We're trying to learn as much as we can about the Soviet Army in order to foster better mutual understanding."

"Ja, ja. I understand," winked the truck driver.

"So why didn't you stay here in '45?"

I didn't immediately understand the question. I just stared at him with a puzzled look.

"Why did you give us back to the Red Army?" the second driver asked.

Neither driver was smiling any longer. Now I knew what he was talking about. The truck driver was referring to a situation that evolved partly from Eisenhower's decision to push toward Leipzig instead of Berlin in the last months of World War II. When the Western Allies reached the Elbe River at Torgau—only sixty miles from Berlin—Ike informed Stalin he wouldn't advance any more in that direction so the Soviets could take Berlin. The result was that the Americans devoted their attention to, and soon occupied a large portion of what was now southwest East Germany. After the war, however, we pulled back to boundaries established at the Yalta Conference in February 1945 by Roosevelt, Churchill and Stalin. From the truck drivers' point of view, the United States abandoned this part of Germany to the Soviets. Had the Americans remained in all the areas we originally occupied, these drivers would be living in West, not East Germany.

There was little I could say. It would do no good to explain to them that both the Yalta concessions to the Soviets and Eisenhower's decision to cede Berlin to the Red Army were still controversial issues among political and military historians today.

"Those things were decided at the very highest levels," I said. "I guess no one knew back then how things would turn out."

"You'll find a lot of us Germans here resent you Americans for that," said the first driver.

"I understand," I said. This was not a topic where much would be accomplished with explanations of World War II diplomacy. Jim opened the back door of the Bronco, reached into our *Kiste* and came up with two packs of Kools cigarettes.

"Here," he said, "Would you like some American cigarettes?"

Both drivers extended their hands and accepted our peace offering.

"*Danke,*" replied the first driver.

"How about a cup of hot coffee on this cold day?" I offered. They both nodded assent. We walked back to our tailgate, wiped out our cups, and filled them with coffee, which we handed over to the truck drivers. They finished it quickly and turned to leave.

"Good hunting," said the second driver. Then both returned to their trucks.

Generally, I found the East German civilian population to be friendly. They were living under very oppressive conditions. Still, at that time they were the eighth-ranked industrial nation in the world. When I saw how much they had accomplished in spite of the Soviet-controlled police state, I began to feel some sympathy for them. I too felt sorry that we had pulled out of this area after the war. I empathized with them when West Germans would visit the East Zone with their Mercedes and BMWs and generally conduct themselves as if they were superior to their East German brothers and sisters. I never heard a West German credit the key role that our Marshall Plan played in helping put West Germany back on its feet.

After the truck drivers left, we resumed our trip to Eisenach, a city near the Intra-German border. Just outside the city is a highway restaurant stop. We pulled in and entered the restaurant only to see teams from the French and British Military Liaison Missions seated at one table. In order to cover the entire country and avoid duplication, each Allied Mission ground tour alternated through what we divided into zones A, B and C. But it was not unusual to find an air team from another Mission in one's zone. That was the case here.

We greeted our comrades-in-arms, sat down at the neighboring table and waited for the waitress. She came out of the kitchen carrying a tray of food and looking down at the floor, apparently not wanting to trip. When she looked up and saw British, French and Americans together in her restaurant, she stopped, got a big smile on her face and exclaimed: "Hallelujah! They've moved the border." We joined in her laughter.

Our last planned target of this tour was to check out a couple of Soviet installations in Eisenach. Because of its proximity to the border, we always monitored activity there when we could. A larger than normal number of troops or vehicles around the installations might indicate preparations for something sinister.

As soon as we left the restaurant and entered Eisenach, the police (VOPO) surveillance picked us up. But we had a trick up our sleeve that would prevent the VOPOs from interfering with our collection. We didn't need to be particularly obvious about what we were doing, since some Soviet installations here and in other towns had what we called "25-mile-an-hour fences." Through a quirk of light and the eye and the brain's ability to process sight, we found that if we drove by the installation at 25 miles per hour, the vertical slats in the fences seemed to disappear, and we could see into the installations as if there were no fences at all. Twenty-five miles per hour was a good speed in the city and raised no suspicions from the VOPOs behind us. Before long, we were on our way back home to Potsdam and Berlin.

Chapter 15
A Class on the U.S. Army

PRENZLAU, 02 August 1977. A USMLM tour was detained in a wooded area in Prenzlau Training Area 446. The tour was escorted to the Prenzlau kommandatura; a protocol was prepared; the tour officer declined to sign. The tour was released at 1235 hours. Soviet behavior was described as correct and courteous. (USMLM Unit History, 1977)

We left Potsdam at 6:00 a.m. on a collection tour in the northeast part of East Germany. We would not reach the area until evening. Our task required that we get as close as possible to the installation we intended to inspect and photograph. To do this, we would have to traverse some rough terrain, some of it by night. An MfS surveillance team picked us up as soon as we left Potsdam. On the Autobahn, however, we were able to outrun their Russian-made Moskvich. When we were a mile or so ahead of the Moskvich, we turned off our taillights and continued at high speed for the next ten miles. There were several places along the way where we could have turned off, so the MfS was unlikely to know for sure which way we had gone.

Just before dark we arrived in our target area and drove into a forest to hide and spend the night in our Bronco. The front seats of Mission vehicles were customized to provide comfort on long drives or for sleeping. We climbed into sleeping bags, reclined the seats and caught some shut-eye. As night fell, the thick, dark forest helped to hide us from almost anyone who might be in the vicinity. The plan was for us to take turns sleeping, while the other stayed awake as a sentry inside the car. Sometimes this worked, sometimes the coziness of the sleeping bag resulted in both of us sleeping at the same time. But of course the doors were always locked.

At 4 a.m., my driver woke me.

"Time to get moving, sir. We still have some rough driving ahead and you said we want to get as close as we can before daylight."

"Right."

We ate a quick breakfast of a sandwich and coffee from our *Kiste*, then departed our forest "inn" and headed toward our target, about twenty miles away. My sergeant donned his night-vision goggles and we drove out of the forest and across a large field. We had only one set of goggles, so I had to trust that my driver knew where he was going. Driving across the open field was no problem. When we entered the woods surrounding the Soviet installation, however, the going got a little dicey. I could see the tree branches reaching out to grab us. I could hear and feel some of them slapping the car as we went by. The distance between trees was sometimes so narrow I was afraid we would hit one.

"Jesus, you think we should go so fast?" I blurted out at one point.

"No sweat, sir. We're only doing about 10 mph. I can see real good with these goggles."

"Remind me next time to bring along a set for myself. This is nerve-racking."

"Trust me, sir."

"I do." And I did. Our drivers were real pros. The vehicles were like extensions of their bodies. In fact, when I first arrived at the Mission, I was sent out with one of the drivers to the Grunewald—the same forest where Teufelsberg, the ASA SIGINT site was located—for a demonstration of the driver's skill in defensive and evasive maneuvering. After the tricks he put our car through, including the 180-degree turns on a dime going forward and backward and the 60-miles-per-hour driving in reverse, I was convinced the Mission drivers knew what they were doing.

The closer we got to the installation, the more difficult the terrain became. By now it wasn't only the trees that worried us, but also the bushes all around us. We slowed to less than 5 mph and often had to stop and try another route. Finally, we came to a thicket that was simply not navigable.

"Let's stop here for a short time," I said, "and wait until we get enough light to see better."

"10-4, sir. I don't want to have to gun the engine to get through any of this. The Sovs might hear us."

We sat there for about half an hour, resuming our breakfast of cold sandwiches, candy bars and hot coffee from our big thermos. As daylight approached, we could see we were in a virtual jungle. Forward, left, and right were closed to passage, except for someone walking. But we weren't close enough to the installation for me to get out and go by foot. In the past, too many Mission officers had been caught outside their cars by Soviets.

"Shit," I said, "I don't know what we can do here."

"Maybe we could back out and go around to the other side of the installation," offered the driver.

"Yeah, but then we run the risk of being seen. If that happens we won't be able to do what we came for and will probably find ourselves on the run."

I was frustrated. After all this time and effort, we had reached a dead end. I didn't relish the thought of going home empty-handed on this target. The driver, I was sure, wouldn't feel good about telling the other drivers he had gotten us into this jam. It really wasn't his fault; I had chosen the route. But he would feel personally responsible. Since we had other targets in the area, I reluctantly decided it would be best to back out and abort this particular mission.

The driver started the engine and turned to look out the back window.

"Son-of-a-bitch, sir. Look what we got here."

I turned and saw a helmeted Soviet on a motorcycle with a sidecar. He was almost upon us. I could see he was wearing a sidearm, so I knew he must be an officer.

"Just what we need," I said. "And us not being able to maneuver."

The Soviet pulled right up to our rear bumper, got off his bike and came to my window. I rolled it down slightly.

"Who are you and what are you doing here?"

"We're American Military Mission members," I answered. "We've gotten lost in these woods."

The Soviet looked around and could tell we hadn't gotten there by accident.

"What were you doing in these woods anyhow?"

"We were looking for a place to rest. We've been driving all night."

The Soviet walked to the rear of the Bronco and stared at the license plate, which had the American flag painted on it and the number 26. He went back to his motorcycle and took out a small notebook.

"He probably has one of the 'alert' cards (See Appendix D) in there telling him to be on the lookout for foreign Military Liaison Mission cars," I said to my driver. "We have the same thing in West Germany. We pass them out to the troops so they can report sightings of any Soviet military liaison teams."

The Soviet put his notebook away and instructed us to back out. He said he would remain behind us until we came to a fork in the path. Then he would lead us to the *komendatura*. He hadn't asked for my pass, so there was still a chance we might get away if we came to a clearing. He had our license number and I'd probably get in trouble with the GSFG HQ if I tried to run now, but it was still a possibility.

We began to back out. When we reached the fork, I had to make a decision. But it looked like the only escape route ran directly toward the installation. So I let the Soviet pull in front and lead us down that road to the *komendatura*, which turned out to be inside the very military installation we were trying to observe.

"We might at least get a look at something in here," I said to my driver. And that we did, but there was nothing of interest. I saw only T-62 tanks, some trucks, and other equipment we already had plenty of information about.

Inside the *komendatura* I was led into a room with a long conference table. I was told to have a seat and was offered a cup of tea. I politely refused. Who knew what might be in it? Even though this was my third clobber, I was uneasy. I could see things were going to be different again this time. If only because it was inside an installation and many people were about. When three officers and one civilian soon appeared and took seats around the table, I didn't know what to expect.

"Tell us who you are." The speaker was a lieutenant colonel with armor insignia on his shoulder boards.

"I'm Major Holbrook from the U.S. Military Liaison Mission. I have every right to be where I was when I was detained. It's not a restricted area."

"You're wrong, Mr. Holbrook." There was that "mister" again. Russians didn't use the term "mister" (*gospodin*) among themselves in contemporary Russian. The term hearkened back to the pre-revolutionary days and was associated with "bourgeois" Russians or foreigners. I felt it was a breach of military courtesy to use the term for brother military officers. And we were, after all, brothers in a way. In all my contacts with foreign military officers, I often found a mutual respect toward duty and one's own country, as well as the responsibilities and dangers of the profession of arms. I even sensed that camaraderie among some regular Soviet officers in the meetings I had with them since my arrival at the Mission. But their habit of not addressing foreign officers by rank irritated me.

"You were in an area that is posted off-limits to Foreign Military Mission personnel," chimed in a major.

"You went past a large sign that says you are not permitted in this area." The civilian said nothing.

The restricted area he referred to was neither a PRA indicated on our maps nor a Temporary Restricted Area (TRA) set up for military exercises. It was an area behind one of the locally generated Mission Restriction Signs (MRS) we Allies didn't recognize. Mission officers never argued about the legality or illegality of the MRSs; we simply ignored them.

"According to my map, we were not in a restricted area," I countered.

"In any case, what were you doing in this area?" asked the lieutenant colonel.

"As I told the officer who detained us, we were looking for a place to rest and we got lost."

The lieutenant colonel looked at me for a few moments and tried to hold back a smile. Then he said, "We want you to sign an *Akt* we've prepared that states you were in a restricted area."

"I can't do that. In the first place, it's wrong. In the second place I won't sign anything."

At this point three more officers came in and sat down. They all whispered to each other. There were now six officers and the civilian seated around the table. The major who had been there when I arrived changed the subject.

"Tell us something about how you became an officer."

"And I'm curious what all that insignia on your uniform stands for," said one of the new arrivals.

The Mission had a liberal policy on what we wore when on tour. The one rule was that it had to be a military uniform, with the Mission patch on the shoulder. Both officer and driver usually dressed the same; sometimes the uniform was dressier than others. It all depended on what the team was going to do during their travels. On this tour I was wearing my "greens"—the relatively dressy class A uniform most U.S. Army officers wear daily in their offices. I had chosen this uniform because I was planning to stay in a hotel one night before we returned to Potsdam and Berlin. I thought it only proper that my driver and I provide a neat, military appearance when dealing with the general public.

"How did you become an officer?" I asked the major. The major looked at the lieutenant colonel, then at the civilian, and then back at me.

"I studied five years at the Moscow Higher Military School," he answered.

"I was promoted directly from staff sergeant to first-lieutenant," I offered.

They wondered how that could be. I proudly told them the Army financed my college and graduate school while I was still on active duty. They said they had never heard anything like that about the American Army. It was their understanding that officers were selected from the wealthy business classes or from military dynasties. While we were talking, other officers entered the room and soon the table was full. We began to exchange information about the differences between military careers in the U.S. and the Soviet Union. I relaxed somewhat. We talked about retirement and pensions, housing allowances, schools for dependents, medical care, pay and promotions. The question of the *Akt* never surfaced again. After all, they knew at the outset I wouldn't sign anything, but it was an exercise they had to go through. The things I was telling them were common, public knowledge, although I'm sure many of them were hearing it for the first time. I too was learning a few things about Soviet Army personnel policies.

"Where did you learn to speak Russian so well?" the civilian asked.

When I stated that my grandfather had spoken Russian (true) around the house (not true; he never lived with us), that seemed to satisfy their curiosity. We moved on to other topics.

"Were you ever in Vietnam?"

"Yes."

"What did you do there?"

"I commanded a reconnaissance detachment with an infantry brigade. You don't need to know any more than that."

"What do you think of war?"

"It's like they say, 'war's hell.' And I'm sure you'll agree that the people who most subscribe to this characterization are professional soldiers. The ones who have to fight the wars." This brought approving murmurs from around the room. It wasn't entirely true, of course, since some military personnel revel in the chance to participate in war. Decorations are easy to come by; promotions are fast. But most of the war veterans I know would agree that the highest calling of a military professional is to prevent war, rather than fight one. As General Eisenhower is purported to have said, "Our job is to work ourselves out of a job."

I drove home the value of the American NCO to our army. I taught them the American expression "Sergeants are the backbone of the Army." It was a subject the Soviet officers had trouble dealing with. In their army—a fully conscripted/draft army—soldiers served for the most part only two years and quickly got out of the service. Junior officers had to perform many of the duties carried out by our senior NCOs. Due to the brutal conditions in their army, it was almost unthinkable for a Soviet soldier to consider reenlisting for more service. During this discussion I reiterated that I myself, the stepson of a lowly railroad worker, had been an NCO, received my higher education through army sponsorship and then was commissioned as an officer.

Nearly two hours passed. Soviet officers had been coming in, staying for a while, and then leaving. The lieutenant colonel, who had originally confronted me and demanded that I sign the *Akt,* left after the first fifteen minutes. It was clear to me that hardly any of these officers knew anything about the American Army other than what they "learned" in political classes. They seemed genuinely curious to know as much as possible about the human aspects of our army. By now I was completely relaxed and found that when the lieutenant colonel returned and told me I could go on my way, I was a little sorry to leave.

When I reached the Bronco, my sergeant searched the expression on my face for any indication I had been mistreated.

"You must've gotten a real grilling in there, sir. I saw *beaucoup* officers going into the *komendatura.*"

"No. In fact, you won't believe what happened. Everyone was eager to find out about how U.S. soldiers lived and what opportunities the army provided its people." I gave my driver some examples of the questions I had been asked.

The Soviets escorted us out of their installation and set us free on Route 198. Now I had three clobbers under my belt, all three benign, but quite different. I wondered whether I had talked too much, but decided no. I had seized an opportunity to inform a small part of the Soviet officer corps about the real American Army. I thought of myself as having briefly replaced their political officer. It was quite likely some of them would share their new knowledge with brother officers. I felt I had made a small dent in the massive problem of misunderstanding between our two armies. Exchanges like the one we just had could do nothing but reduce the damage from Soviet disinformation and the prejudices we both held about the other.

Chapter 16
Passage Prohibited!

Whenever we set out to collect intelligence information on the Soviet or East German armies, we expected our adversaries to place certain obstacles in our way. One such obstacle was surveillance, which could be very unnerving at times.

For example, imagine, you're driving along a highway here in the United States, minding your own business, when a police car suddenly appears behind you. It follows you for several miles, while other cars pass both of you (you're certainly going under the speed limit by now). You enter a town and pull into a gas station to fill up. The police car also pulls in and simply parks nearby. When you depart, it departs, once again on your tail. You're probably a little nervous by now.

Now imagine driving in hostile territory and planning to steal something from a factory or a government facility. (One of the paradoxes of intelligence is that it requires collectors to do many things that would be illegal in our own country. Lying and stealing were part of our tradecraft.) The police car is still with you. You certainly find it a bit nerve-racking, to say the least. Now, if you have created this image in your mind, your pulse should be racing a little.

This gives you an idea what it was like for Mission personnel when they came under surveillance for the first time in East Germany. I've commented in earlier chapters about surveillance and what we did to evade it on some Mission tours I took. Here we look at the larger surveillance problem.

Early on in the history of the Allied Missions, Soviet agents of the Ministry of Internal Affairs (MVD), another precursor of the KGB, conducted discreet surveillance of the Military Missions. Upon declaration of the German Democratic Republic in 1949, and especially after the Soviet Union extended full diplomatic recognition in 1955, the responsibility for Allied Mission surveillance began to shift to the East German Ministry of State Security (MfS).

Over the years, MfS surveillance of Mission vehicles was uneven. At times, it was simple—perhaps one low-powered East German car, which was easy to outrun. At other times, it was more sophisticated. But it almost always was more overt and intrusive than earlier Soviet surveillance. At times, it appeared that a central operations center was coordinating surveillance of Mission vehicles. On other occasions, tour surveillance seemed to be inexplicably amateurish and haphazard. The 1969 USMLM Unit History suggested that during that year, the MfS and VOPO agencies were working together and using radio communications to pass the Mission vehicles from one jurisdiction to another. Periodic announcements were even heard on public radio broadcasts requesting citizens to immediately report sightings of Mission vehicles to the local VOPO.

In addition to the assistance of the easily identified East German police, the MfS was aided by Grenzpolizei (border police), Bereitschaftspolizei (alert police), Transportpolizei (railway police), augmented by political officials, foresters, business managers, and so-called "do-gooder" citizens.

For the most part, the surveillance was what we call "overt," that is, MfS or VOPO teams remained as close as they could to Mission vehicles. They wanted us to know they were there. We had no doubt who they were and why they were following us. Their purpose at those times was to intimidate us and thus prevent us from carrying out our intelligence tasks. To a certain extent, they were successful in this regard if we hadn't been able to shake them along the way. (One exception was the VOPO surveillance in Eisenach I related in Chapter 14, where we were able to tool along and do our job with the VOPOs on our tail, thanks to the 25-mile-an-hour fences.)

When we parked our cars in a city to walk around and browse in the stores or to conduct sightseeing, it is quite possible the foot surveillance was "covert." We usually didn't pay much attention to surveillance on those occasions, since we were not engaged in any illicit activities. In fact, except for SANDDUNE operations (See Chapters 17 and 18), we conducted almost all of our intelligence collection activities from vehicles. The few times we might be in a restaurant or hotel and, thus, subject to close-up *Stasi* surveillance, it is far from certain the *Stasi* were very good at their job. Judging from excerpts of my partial MfS dossier, I've concluded there must have been a lot of 'filling in the blanks' by *Stasi* agents just to get a report filed. (See Appendix F.)

Photo 17: One of the times we successfully eluded surveillance and avoided a clobber. My driver, Sergeant Jim Rice, surveys the damage we incurred during the chase.

The standard surveillance vehicles during my time at the Mission were the East German Wartburg and the Soviet-made Moskvich or Fiat, the Lada. Earlier, according to the 1965 Unit History, the MfS sometimes used Mercedes and BMWs. Occasionally, the MfS would mount well-organized surveillance by using packs of East German cars equipped with two-way radios. In late 1965, one Mission team reported 30 vehicles in a single surveillance pack. On one of my trips in northern East Germany, we were surveilled by a total of five MfS cars, some of which were waiting for us at Autobahn overpasses. If surveillants used Western vehicles, which they rarely did, they might be able to keep up with us when we were on the main highways. Using East German cars, however, also had its advantages; the cars were less conspicuous in East German traffic.

When surveilled by a Russian Volga, we suspected the occupants of being Soviet KGB. We had no way of knowing, however, unless for some reason we would get a chance to talk to the narks in a restaurant or hotel. I don't think it was ever determined definitively that the KGB took part in vehicular surveillance during the 1970s. By 1969, according to the USMLM Unit History, "surveillance by Soviet or East German military personnel [was] rarely encountered."

Three things allowed us to overcome the stress and intimidation that a normal person would feel when subjected to obvious police car surveillance. First, it soon became so common that we got used to it. Second, we could often get away anytime we chose. Third, we recognized we were up to no good in their eyes, and they were only doing their job. Unlike you the reader, driving along a U.S. highway, we were planning to photograph Soviet or East German secret facilities and to steal whatever we could from their training areas or installations.

Other obstacles to our intelligence collection were restricted areas the Soviets created for us. These restricted areas came about, in part, because all the Missions—the Allies in East Germany and the Soviets in West Germany—continually violated one of the important provisions of the agreements setting up the Missions in 1946 and 1947. Article 10 of the Huebner-Malinin Agreement (Appendix A), for example, stated that members of each Mission would be granted "complete freedom of travel wherever and whenever it will be desired over territory and roads in both zones, *except places of disposition of military units*, without escort or supervision." [Italics added] As the importance and frequency of intelligence collection grew during those first post-war years, staying away from military units and their installations became...well, simply impractical. Nonetheless, had all Missions observed their official agreements with each other, there would have been no need for the restricted areas. But then there would also have been no added value to the presence of the Military Liaison Missions in each other's territories.

In our protests, we often cited the first and last part of that provision of the Huebner-Malinin Agreement, to wit: "complete freedom of travel wherever and whenever it will be desired over territory and roads in both zones... without escort or supervision." Whenever we were detained, the Soviets, on the other hand, used the middle part of the sentence—"except places of disposition of military units."

Areas in which large concentrations of military units or extensive training areas were located were designated Permanent Restricted Areas (PRA) and were marked on maps the Soviet army headquarters provided the Allied Missions (See Map 2). Temporary Restricted Areas (TRA) were often established several times a year for military exercises and usually connected two or more PRAs.

The Soviets imposed the first PRAs in 1951. Not long after that, the Allies did the same in West Germany. Compared to those of later years, the first Soviet PRAs caused the Missions little concern. They included the Intra-German border area, an area that extended along the frontier with Czechoslovakia, and one small section of East Germany east of Magdeburg that extended south to Halle. But in January 1957, according to *The Story of BRIXMIS*, "without any previous warning," the Allied Missions received new and "greatly enlarged" PRA maps. By 1960, there were about 16 PRAs.

At times in USMLM's history, violations of PRAs and TRAs did occur (Fahey writes: "Generally the maps [of TRAs] were ignored and did not keep us from following Soviet military movements.") By the mid-1970s, however, USMLM personnel were very careful not to enter PRAs or TRAs except with approval from the Soviets—for example to recover aircraft and crews after accidents or shoot-downs, or to visit U.S. citizens in hospitals. BRIXMIS followed the same rule in that their official policy was never intentionally to violate PRAs.

Staying out of the official restricted areas was also a smart move on the part of Mission personnel. In 1971, 12 Soviet soldiers caught a USMLM team in a PRA. The soldiers threw the Mission personnel to the ground and tied their hands. The Soviets then proceeded to remove all the equipment from the Mission vehicle, including camera equipment, two-way radios, binoculars, a tape recorder, maps, an aircraft identification book, and a notebook. Most of the equipment was never returned to the Mission.

By the 1970s, traveling in a good one third of East Germany was denied to the Allied Missions because of the placement of PRAs. Many highways were inaccessible because they went through PRAs. On one occasion, I fell asleep in the car when we were headed north. My driver took a wrong turn, or didn't make a turn he should have, and when I woke up, we were in the middle of the Neu

Brandenburg PRA. I immediately had the driver speed up so we could exit the other end of the PRA as soon as possible.

Mission Restriction Signs (MRSs) presented a different story altogether. The Soviets and East Germans placed them in military training areas and near military facilities that were not located in PRAs. The first MRSs were seen also in 1951. In 1955 BRIXMIS had recorded 450 of them. By 1964, there were about 2,500 of them throughout East Germany. The number increased with each year. By 1965, there were 3,000; by 1971, 7,000; and by 1978, USMLM estimated there were approximately 10,000 such signs. Until January 1958, the signs were often crude, some containing comical errors. For example, *The Story of BRIXMIS* contains a picture of one sign that in Russian, German, and French states photography is not allowed; but in English (at the top of the sign!) it reads "Taking pictures is allowed."

In January 1958, BRIXMIS historians report that "all existing MRSs (more than 1,000) were replaced by brand new signs of identical pattern with the wording in black in four languages on a white board mounted on a red post." All the MRSs now read: "ATTENTION! PASSAGE OF MEMBERS OF FOREIGN MILITARY LIAISON MISSIONS PROHIBITED!" in English, French, Russian and German. (*The Story of BRIXMIS* contains an interesting suggestion that the first to post Mission Restriction Signs was the British Army on the Rhine against SOXMIS in West Germany. The Soviets may have simply reciprocated with their own version.)

USMLM and the other Allied Mission tours usually ignored MRSs. More accurately, we ignored their messages and often brazenly went behind the signs. As mentioned previously, we did honor the PRAs, but the MRSs were, in our view, a violation of the "unspoken rules of engagement." Even a KGB pamphlet and memorandum giving instructions for handling Allied Missions during detentions do not mention MRSs. (See Appendixes C and D.)

Early in the history of MRSs, however, the Soviets took umbrage at our violations. In October 1958, according to *The Story of BRIXMIS*, the Chief of Staff at the Soviet Headquarters issued an ultimatum to the Missions. He declared that the signs "were to be obeyed. In the event of these orders being disobeyed, the Chiefs of the Allied Liaison Missions will be held personally responsible by my Commander in Chief." His threat carried little weight.

In many ways, MRSs were counterproductive for the Soviets. They provided us with tip-offs as to where military facilities or activities were. We would be driving along a side road, see a sign and say, "Whoa! Must be something over there. Let's check it out."

The notoriety of the MRSs for us at the Allied Missions created several disrespectful actions. According to Geraghty's *BRIXMIS*, a former BRIXMIS Chief, the Duke of Norfolk, suggested a necktie he made with little MRSs depicted on it. All the Allied Missions acquired these ties made by "the gentleman's tailor of Savile Row." When I read Geraghty's statement, I looked at the label of my own MRS tie. It reads "Gieves & Hawkes, Ltd of Savile Row, London." Former French Missionary Daniel Trastour, in his *La guerre sans armes*, reports the French

Mission officers sometimes wore their MRS ties with their uniforms to social functions with the Soviets. According to Trastour, the Soviets never really caught on, thinking the little white and red symbols on the blue ties were simply some form of French adornment.

MRSs also provided good souvenirs. The 1971 USMLM Unit History reports that during the last four months of the year, USMLM tours collected 125 signs. In 1976, for the U.S. Bicentennial Fourth of July picnic at the Potsdam House, MRSs were covered with foil and used as trays upon which all the decorated cakes were placed. The Soviets always came to this picnic and brought their families. Imagine the surprise if a Soviet had cut through the tin foil. He would have seen one of his own MRS signs!

ATTENTION! PASSAGE OF MEMBERS
OF FOREIGN   MILITARY   LIAISON
MISSIONS   **PROHIBITED!**

ATTENTION! PASSAGE AUX
MEMBRES des MISSIONS MILITAIRES
ETRANGERES de **LIAISON** est **INTERDIT!**

ПРОЕЗД   ЧЛЕНАМ   ИНОСТРАННЫХ
ВОЕННЫХ МИССИЙ
СВЯЗИ ЗАПРЕШЕН!

Durchfahrt für das Personal der
ausländischen Militärverbindungs-
Missionen ist VERBOTEN!

Photo 18: Military Restriction Sign (MRS)

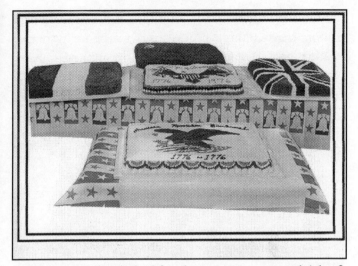

Photo 19: Cakes baked for the U.S. Bicentennial 4th of July party at Potsdam House. Beneath each cake is an MRS wrapped in foil.

At USMLM, once it was established that an officer or NCO had been behind an MRS on a collection tour, he was awarded one of the MRS neckties. We also kept a sign at our Berlin headquarters for visiting dignitaries. After our standard briefing, we would ask the visitor to come up to the front of the room. Then we would hold up an MRS in front of him or her and explain that he or she had now been "behind an MRS," so was qualified to receive one of our neckties. A former USMLM Chief told a researcher that: "There was a period when every tour officer was required to bring back a sign. Almost every tour type, past and present, has an MRS in mint condition displayed prominently somewhere in his home." I have mine, although it isn't in mint condition.

During one tour, Staff Sergeant Germaine and I were driving cross-country, headed back to the highway that would take us to Potsdam. By this time, we had probably been behind a dozen MRSs, but we had been focused on our collection mission, rather than on signs. At the moment we were relaxed.

"Look at that old MRS, Ralph," I said, pointing to a wooden sign high on a red stake. We slowed down and stopped a few feet away.

"You got one yet, sir?" he asked.

"No, as a matter of fact."

"That looks like an antique."

He was referring to the fact that, unlike almost all the MRSs around East Germany at the time, made from thin sheets of steel, this one was made of wooden boards. The wording was standard, and the sign was attached securely by screws and nails to the red stake.

"I don't think I can reach it, Ralph."

"No problem, sir." Ralph turned the motor off and jumped out of the car. In a flash, he grabbed tools from the trunk and was working at loosening the sign.

"Try to keep it in one piece," I said as I began taking photographs of each step he made in removing the sign.

"Yeah, I know. It's a bit more fragile than the metal signs," he answered.

That MRS now has four short legs appended to it and makes an interesting little coffee table in my study.

**Photos 20, 21, 22: Staff Sergeant Ralph Germaine
retrieves an MRS for me.**

CHAPTER 17
TRASH RUNS

Sneaking along a trail through a forest illuminated only by a full moon on a surreptitious mission would make anyone nervous. Although we had done this several times before, I could feel the adrenalin pumping and my muscles tightening. We were attempting to reach a Soviet trash dump without attracting the attention of the German population or Soviet troops. Thanks to the full moon, we were able to navigate the trail leading to the dump without the use of headlights or night-vision gear. Although the dump was close to the highway running past the Soviet installation, we had chosen to approach it from the opposite direction, a few miles from the installation, so the forest would cover our movement. An hour had passed since we left the main highway and we were getting close. There was no snow yet, but the temperature was well below freezing and the ground was firm.

I had mixed feelings about digging around in trash dumps. There were always rats screeching and scurrying around, plus the stink from all sorts of slimy, decaying trash, including hazardous waste. At least this dump would be better than the one outside the Soviet hospital in

Beelitz! Now that everything was frozen, it might not be so bad tonight. And, besides, the take was almost always worth any discomfort we suffered.

My driver was very quiet as he concentrated on maneuvering our vehicle. There was no reason for us to discuss what we were going to do. We had prepared for this stop, along with other collection assignments on this tour before we left Berlin, and now everything would be pretty routine—as long as nothing went wrong. The sergeant would stay near the car and watch for interlopers, while I did my thing.

He drove the car out of the woods into the clearing used for the trash dump. First phase successful. A line of trees obstructed the view of the dump from the Soviet garrison across the road. I had ridden many times past this spot and had seen the telltale signs of a trash dump— mounds of old propaganda signs, discarded equipment and papers. With car windows down, and the wind blowing just right, even an inexperienced nose could tell there was a trash dump nearby. I marked the site on my map and resolved to visit it sometime at night. The trail we had used to get here continued past the pile of rubbish and out onto the highway.

"Pull up over there," I instructed the driver. "We'll turn the car around so it's headed back into the woods, in case someone comes in off the road. Watch out for the left side."

"No problem, sir."

He maneuvered the car slowly along the narrow path between the piles of trash on the right and a deep gully on the left. I was a little nervous about the gully.

"Pull up here and turn around."

"Got it, sir." Using a gap between trash piles, the driver negotiated the forward-backward movements necessary to get the Opel turned around.

"Let's stop beside the middle pile," I said. "It's tall enough that we can hide behind it, in case anyone can see through the trees. But watch that gully."

The sergeant moved the car forward slowly. From his side, it was not easy to judge how much room there was on the right—now the gully side. I was looking at the trash piles, already forming my search strategy. Mentally overlaying a grid on the middle pile, I felt like an archeologist about to begin a dig. I always started from the bottom of a pile and worked my way around the outside. Not only was this the easiest and safest, but also there was always a chance I would find something freshly discarded that would need immediate exploitation. If so, it could be valuable enough to call it a day and head back to Berlin without having to dig through the rest of the trash. Someone else, or I myself, could come back another day to pick up where I had left off. I had found some interesting personal journals once. Maybe tonight I would get lucky again.

Suddenly, the driver slammed on the brakes, but the car jerked forward. I shot a glance at him and then looked out my window. I found myself gazing down into the 30-foot gully. The right front part of the car was tilting in that direction.

"Shit. Don't move."

"Don't *you* move, sir! The right front tire has slipped off the path. I'm going to try to back up."

"Take it nice and easy. Don't rev the engine. We don't want anyone to hear."

As the driver shifted into reverse, the car gave a slight groan and seemed to wobble. "This is one of our front-wheel drives," the driver said, "but I've only got the left drive wheel left, sir. It doesn't look like it's enough to move the car. We may have bottomed out on your side."

"Then stop," I said hurriedly. "Don't do anything. Let me think."

Neither of us spoke for a few seconds. Although during critical situations the sergeant was responsible for handling the car, the officer always had to make the final decision about what actions to take. I had a formula for making quick decisions when it appeared the Soviets were about to detain us. But this was a different kind of crisis, so I had to consider several new options. Continue to try to back out? Crawl over the seat and get out on the left rear door and push, while the driver remained at the wheel? But I might shake the car too much getting out. If we could both get out of the car, we could get the deadman from the trunk and winch the car backwards. Lord knows, I had done that enough times in mud and snow! In the end, that seemed to be the only workable solution. Just so long as we could get out of the car without it tipping into the gully.

"Put the emergency brake on and open your door. We're both going to try to get out your side. While you slide slowly out, I'll be sliding in your direction. If I can make it to your seat, we should be o.k. Then we'll get the deadman and winch the car back. But move very slowly."

"O.K., sir. Here I go."

He opened his door and began to slide out. I moved in tandem with him. The car creaked some, but maintained its position. I was dressed in a heavy wool uniform and found it difficult to slide behind the steering wheel into the driver's seat. My driver was out, waiting on the path. I continued to move carefully to my left, finally getting out to join him. We stood there for a few seconds surveying the situation. The sergeant was about to say something, when I held up my hand.

"Shhh! Listen! What's that?" I whispered.

Male voices floated through the trees. We could hear not only voices, but also distinct words. In Russian.

"... more days, Vanya. And we're outta here."

"And none too soon, Vova. I can't ... this army shit."

"What ... if you ... Tanya..."

"My mother wrote ... apartment..."

The words were breaking up in the light wind, but there was no doubt I was listening to the guards in the towers of the Soviet garrison. Although they were at least 200 feet away, sometimes it sounded like the distance was only 25 feet. I knew the atmosphere plays tricks with sound. I remembered sometimes being able to understand what people were saying as they walked along the road a hundred feet behind my apartment in Berlin.

"It's the Soviet guards," I whispered. "They're talking about getting out this spring and going home. I hope to hell they can't hear us. Maybe the sound is carrying only in our direction. We're going to have to be really careful with the deadman."

Generally, if there were a tree nearby, the winch would be attached to it. If there were no fixed objects around, as was the case tonight, we would have to make our own by using the deadman. The deadman became the unmovable object by anchoring it in the ground with a metal stake. For long distances, you dragged the car until it reached the deadman, then you picked up the deadman, moved it, winched again, picked it up, moved it, winched again until the car was on hard surface again.

"What're we gonna do, sir?"

"We'll have to pound the stake only when the wind is blowing and hope the sound doesn't carry in the direction of the garrison."

The sergeant carefully opened the trunk. Inside was a pile of blankets, some food, a Coleman stove, a winch, a mallet, and our "savior," the deadman. Both of us spoke in whispers.

"We're gonna have a hell of a time getting the stake into the ground, sir. It's frozen, and we're gonna make noise with the mallet."

"I know. But it's only a surface freeze. All we have to do is winch back about two feet. Let's get started and see what happens."

The deadman was heavy; we took hold of it, lifted it quietly out of the trunk, and carried it to a spot where it could be anchored. My driver placed the stake in the hole through the deadman and waited for my cue. When a breeze came up, I signaled for him to start.

C-L-A-A-A-N-K!

The shrill sound of metal striking metal reverberated through the cold night.

"Stop!" I quickly whispered, raising my hand. We stood there, holding our breath and listening for a sign the Soviet guards had heard the noise. Silence. I wondered whether the guards stopped talking only to listen more closely? Or did they just accept the noise as a sound of the night? They *must* have heard the clank.

After a few moments, I looked at my sergeant.

"This isn't going to work. It's just too loud. If they didn't hear us this time, they will sooner or later."

"How about we fold up a blanket and put it on top of the stake," the driver suggested. "That'll muffle the noise."

"Good idea. How many do we have?"

The sergeant laid the mallet down and went over to the car. When he returned, he was carrying two army blankets. He folded one over and placed it atop the stake.

"Here, you hold this, sir. I'll give it another hit."

"O.K. I hope your aim's good," I said as I let out a nervous chuckle. "Let's wait for the wind..."

A few moments later the mallet came down on the blanket and stake.

K-F-F-F-F-T.

He stopped. We looked down at the deadman and smiled with relief at each other. The stake hadn't gone very far into the frozen ground, but it had started to penetrate the surface and the sound had been well muffled. Now it would be only a matter of time. We had solved our problem. Or, I admitted to myself, my driver had solved our problem.

"O.K. By George, I think we've got it," I said, using a pet phrase from my favorite movie, *My Fair Lady*. "Let's get started. You pound for a while, while I hold. Then we'll switch. I don't think we even have to wait for the wind."

K-F-F-F-F-T.

K-F-F-F-F-T.

K-F-F-F-F-T.

C-L-A-A-A-N-K!

"Damn, sir! The top of the stake has worn through the blanket. We'll have to use both of them." But before I could respond, Russian voices again pierced the night.

"What was that?" The question shot through the trees. "Vanya, ... anything? Vanya!"

"Quiet! Listen, Vova!"

Silence in the trash dump. My driver and I stopped breathing. Silence from the guard towers. Then once again, the Russian.

"I ... noise across the road. Did you?"

"I'm not sure, I think.... Don't say... minutes."

The discussion between the two Russian sentries stretched beyond the time we could hold our breath. I looked down at the stake in the deadman. It didn't seem to be deep enough in the ground to hold the metal plate firmly enough if we tried to winch the car backwards. We had to do something. I didn't want to just sit there and I didn't want to start making noise again.

The last thing I wanted was to be caught red-handed. To be caught collecting documents from a trash dump would not only be embarrassing on a personal level, it could threaten the entire trash collection effort. The Soviets might become wise to the fact that we were exploiting their rubbish for intelligence purposes. Up to now, they seemed to have assumed we wouldn't go near such filthy deposits and they were free to throw out whatever they wanted. The Soviets hadn't caught us in this activity so far. I certainly didn't want to be the first. (A couple of years earlier, a tour officer working a trash dump returned to find his driver and vehicle surrounded by MfS agents. They apparently never guessed what he was up to, as he was later charged only with "being in a restricted area.")

An idea occurred to me. Perhaps we should gather up our equipment and hide it back in the trunk. Then I would walk over to the Soviet installation, knock on the gate, and ask for assistance with our vehicle. I would tell them we had pulled off the road to relieve ourselves and got stuck. It was a risky plan, first of all because the Soviets would not likely believe me. If that were the case, we would certainly be detained. But then again, they might believe me. Without proof of any wrongdoing, they might just help us out, and we would be on our way back to Berlin.

The other course of action was to wait a reasonable time until the Soviet guards decided that whatever the noise, it was a natural sound of the night and, in any case, could no longer be heard. Then we would increase the padding on the top of the stake and continue our task of setting the deadman so we could winch the car.

That's the course I opted for. After about ten minutes, we refolded the blanket and added the second blanket. The driver then began to pound the stake again, starting slowly.

K-K-F-F-T-T-T.

K-K-F-F-T-T-T.

K-K-F-F-T-T-T.

So far so good. From time to time we stopped and checked the underside of the blanket. A new hole was forming, but we refolded the blanket. After about 15 minutes, we determined the stake was solidly in the ground. We then proceeded to rig the winch and crank the car backwards. This operation made very little noise.

I heard no more ominous conversations from the Soviet sentries. We cranked like hell, successfully pulling the car back onto the path. I believed we had dodged a bullet, so to speak, and decided to abort the collection mission here. There was a chance the Soviet guards had reported the earlier "clank" to their duty officer and a patrol would be sent out to investigate. We put everything away, got back in the car, and drove back out on the trail we had come in on. Daylight was approaching and we were able to travel a little faster. It was time to move on to the next target.

On another occasion, Staff Sergeant Germaine and I drove an olive drab Opel to Leipzig to, among other things, check out the conditions and supplies of goods in the stores. Leipzig was a major commercial center of the GDR, with a population of nearly half a million people. It appeared to us the residents were somewhat better off here than in many towns we visited. Leipzig has hosted international trade fairs since the Middle Ages. Mission officers often visited these semiannual fairs to photograph exhibits and pick up valuable literature on the newest forms of technology in the GDR.

There was one shop I remember particularly well. It was a music store near the 950-year-old Church of St. Nicholas, where I could buy classical music LPs for 12 East Marks. That equated to about $1.20 in U.S. dollars. Herr Haas's music store and the pipe shop in Erfurt were about the only places I shopped in East Germany.

More important than our survey of the stores, however, was the 241st Guards Motorized Rifle Regiment that was billeted outside of town. The installation was pretty much out in the open, so the only time it could be approached safely was at night. That's why we selected an olive drab car. It was harder to detect at night. Although it got dark early, our planned departure from our hotel was delayed by the appearance of the Klaus I mentioned in Chapter 13. As I stated there, we were able to get out of the hotel undetected in the middle of the night and head for the 241st.

When we turned onto the dirt road that led to the installation, I instructed my driver to turn on the "motorcycle" lights. With the flip of a couple switches, we displayed only one headlight and one taillight. To observers we now appeared to be a motorcycle. As we approached the installation, we turned off all lights and donned night-vision goggles. The installation was dark. From what we could see, it also appeared relatively empty of military vehicles and equipment.

"Looks like we picked the right night," I said to Sergeant Germaine.

"Yeah," he responded, "Not gonna complain about there not being any Sovs around."

Just to the north of the installation we pulled off the road into a large trash area. There were several mounds in the dump and I figured the ones farthest from the installation would probably be the most likely to yield the freshest material.

"Pull up here behind this mound," I said. "It's high enough to cover us from any guard post in the installation's guard towers."

No vehicles had followed us since we turned off the highway onto the well-packed dirt road, and we didn't see any civilians in the trash area. There was no reason to dally, however, so I took the night-vision goggles off and laid them on the dashboard, put on gloves, took a flashlight and a plastic bag, and got out of the vehicle. The driver turned the vehicle around so it pointed toward the road in case we had to leave quickly.

It was mid-November and many of the soldiers and officers had rotated back to the Soviet Union. There was a good chance they had thrown out some of their personal belongings, letters or journals as they packed for home. That was indeed the case. I found several notebooks in which officers had made political notes. In addition to the notes, however, were various scribblings about other officers in the regiment. I came across pictures of privates and sergeants clowning for the camera. One picture was of an attractive girl. On the back was written "Natasha." I wondered why it had been thrown away. Perhaps it was a "Dear Ivan" case. (Ivan is the Russian equivalent of John; in Old Russian it was spelled Ioann.)

Someone had even thrown out training schedules and charts. I took the charts straight back to the vehicle and put them in the trunk because they were too big for my plastic bag. A radio manual marked "*Dlya sluzhebnogo potrebleniya*" (For Official Use Only) was also in the trash.

We had been in the trash dump for over an hour when suddenly a faint light passed across my face. I looked up and saw the light beam move across the trash area toward the regiment's installation. I quickly returned to our vehicle.

"Did you see that?" I asked Ralph.

"Yes, sir. It came from over there in the north."

We put on our night-vision goggles and surveyed the landscape to the north. In the distance we could see faint lights. Not headlights, but rather what appeared to be vehicle running lights. While we were looking in that direction the light beam swept by us again, this time causing a flare-up in our goggles that temporarily blinded us.

"Jesus. Someone's using a searchlight," I said, as we both jerked our goggles off.

"You got that right, sir. And if you look closely you'll see there's a column of vehicles coming our way."

"You think we can get out of here?" I asked. "On second thought, get the car back behind this mound. It'll shield us from the column."

Sergeant Germaine jumped into the Opel and backed it behind the pile of trash that was about ten feet high. The searchlight passed by us again. At least it didn't stop, but continued its sweep on past the installation. We could see the column was quite long.

"I think we know now why the installation seemed so lifeless," Ralph said.

"Yeah, this might be the entire regiment."

"I'm going to put an army blanket over the windshield so it doesn't reflect any light, just in case," Ralph volunteered.

"Good idea."

The Opel's olive drab paint covered all metal surfaces of the car, including the bumpers. It was a color that was similar to that of Soviet vehicles. I decided we should stay put, partly because the column was on the road we needed for our egress and partly because there was no need to risk "running the column." Running columns was a bit dicey since a Soviet vehicle could pull out at any time and there wouldn't be any road left. If that didn't cause an accident, it at least increased our chances of being stopped and detained. The gain didn't justify the risk this time, since we already knew who the column must be. Besides, this column would pass in front of us. We wouldn't be able to get any vehicle registration numbers (VRN) in the dark, but with our night-vision goggles on, we could identify some of the vehicles and count the ones we couldn't identify.

"Jesus, sir. It's a long one. I can't see the end yet."

"It's probably the entire regiment," I repeated. "They may have been training in the Grimma or Brandis PRAs. If so, they shouldn't have many vehicles tarped since they wouldn't have to travel the main highway for very long. And watch out for that searchlight."

By now we could follow the light as it swept around so when we saw it coming we removed our goggles and slipped back behind the trash mound. We began to make out individual vehicles. They were traveling in a non-combat formation, in battalion units. I turned on my pocket tape recorder and began to speak into it, giving the numbers and types of vehicles I could identify.

"You keep an eye on our full 360 degrees," I told Sergeant Germaine. "I'll record what I see."

The column was quite close now. The first vehicles began to pass us by. The searchlight continued to sweep about 270 degrees before it started back in the other direction. It stopped when the vehicle on which it was mounted approached the gate of the installation. Fortunately, during this time, the light beam never stopped on the trash pile. By the time the full column had entered the installation, I had counted 35 T-62 tanks, 45 BRDM combat reconnaissance vehicles, 95 BMP combat infantry vehicles, seven BTR-60 armored personnel carriers, six 122mm self-propelled artillery pieces, two ZSU-23-4 anti-aircraft vehicles, and 18 tarped vehicles that were probably SA-7 and SA-9 surface-to-air missile launchers.

"No doubt about it," I said, "the whole damn regiment. Short a few things, but enough to make up a regiment."

"You think we should stay put after they're settled in?" Ralph asked.

"No, we'll wait for a little while, just to make sure there aren't any stragglers and then take off. We already have plenty of material."

The fact that the 241st had more or less dropped into our hands, most certainly having come back from a training exercise, meant that our report would be good information for the SIGINT people at Teufelsberg. If they were monitoring the exercise's radio communications, and had collected call signs that were yet unidentified, our information would help considerably in their analysis. More importantly, however, we would be able to provide "collateral" information that the exercise took place. This meant reports of the 241st being involved in an exercise could be dispatched with a lower security classification and could be more widely distributed. This was one of the valuable advantages of USMLM reports. SIGINT and other clandestine collection means carried very high security classifications. In order to use the information without compromising the source, it was necessary, if possible, to obtain similar intelligence information— collateral—from other not-so-sensitive sources. The Mission was an excellent source for collateral information on GSFG.

Chapter 18
Project "SANDDUNE"

The two episodes in the previous chapter were a small part of a much larger operation just beginning to develop fully in 1976-77. The reader must wonder why a U.S. Army officer would be mucking around in a trash dump. Didn't the United States have other collection efforts that could obtain the information we found there? The short answer is "no."

Since 1947, USMLM had fielded teams that were primarily interested in identification of units and military hardware, in addition to the ever-present need to monitor the level of Soviet and East German military activity for Indications of Hostilities purposes. To this end, we observed, identified, and photographed military columns, installations, training exercises, and the loading and offloading of military equipment on trains. In this way we were able to establish order of battle (OB) and the introduction and training of personnel for new equipment brought in from the Soviet Union. However, a serious gap existed in our intelligence information—a gap of national intelligence proportions.

In his book *Great True Spy Stories*, Allen Dulles wrote:

> If an intelligence service wants to do more than count the number of the enemy and his cannon... it must do more than hide in the bushes and look over the fence, or even look down from high-flying planes and satellites. It has to get inside the enemy's headquarters and listen to conversations. It must steal important plans or documents.

Our attachés in Moscow couldn't fill that need, nor could our multibillion-dollar, national technical collection assets, with the exception of some valuable information gleaned from SIGINT. During my first assignment in Berlin, as an enlisted man at the 78th Special Operations Unit, we were getting inside the "enemy's headquarters" when we intercepted telephone and radio communications of the Soviet Army. But many details about the inner workings of the Soviet and East German armies remained unknown. Ideally, the United States would have agents who had penetrated these military installations. But after 1947, U.S. and British intelligence services found it next to impossible to run agents in Soviet-occupied East Germany.

The precious few times we had the opportunity to talk with Soviet soldiers or officers occurred during the occasional stop at a traffic controller post, some social functions, and, of course, those times when we were detained by the Soviets. Little of real intelligence value could be obtained during those types of meetings. The Soviet soldiers serving as traffic controllers were quite ignorant of what was going on in the Soviet Army. At best, they could tell us only whether there were military columns in the area and what direction they were heading. (Some traffic controllers actually mistook us for Soviet military, especially when we were in Ford Broncos.) Soviet officers present during clobbers usually didn't discuss anything but our alleged infractions or "spying" activities. At social functions, the most we could glean from our contacts was biographical information on the officers who attended the events. What was going on inside the Soviet Army was inaccessible to us.

Project SANDDUNE was an effort to meet this demand for inside information, to find and collect Soviet documents or materiel. Despite their personnel security attitude of near-paranoiac proportions, the Soviets were careless about what they did with their trash. Very often there was no central refuse service, and the Soviets simply discarded their trash wherever they chose. Sometimes this would be just over their installation walls. Other times, there was a central trash dump not too far from the installation. This trash provided some information about the GSFG units that we wouldn't have been able to obtain unless we had contacts within an installation. That, of course, we did not.

Mission personnel were overt intelligence collectors. USMLM teams collected information themselves; we didn't "run"—that is, hire or otherwise use others—to do our intelligence work. Our resorting to rummaging through trash piles was almost an act of desperation, a "field expedient." Trash collection and analysis were just about our only possibility of finding out what was going on inside the Soviet military units.

Almost anything we found had some value for intelligence analysts. David Stafford writes that "information on the USSR was so hard to come by that the lowest, dog-faced private deserter was considered a valuable source." The dearth of our intelligence on the inner workings of GSFG is illustrated by the fact that when I once found a political notebook that listed the number of soldiers in a motorized rifle squad, it was considered hot news in our ground force intelligence community. But that was nothing compared to what the Mission would eventually garner from Project SANDDUNE.

Project SANDDUNE evolved over the years from random efforts by Mission officers picking up items left behind by Soviets in training areas. Training areas were opportunity collection targets; they produced discarded food cans and an occasional piece of clothing or equipment, such as a gas mask or piece of a radio set.

The earliest official reference to trash dump visits by USMLM teams is found in the 1964 USMLM Unit History. When our officers, such as Captain Nick Troyan, began to use their Russian language skills to sort and cull items in trash dumps, then translate them back at the Berlin Operations Center, the Mission discovered they had come upon documents and exhibits of important intelligence value.

What was to become project SANDDUNE owes much to the alertness of a driver/NCO. Captain Troyan told me several years later that his interest was first piqued when his driver, Staff Sergeant Robert Bollinger, called his attention to a blue beret (worn by Soviet airborne troops) and some notebooks in Russian and English. Sergeant Bollinger informed Troyan they were in a small trash dump, but reminded him they had passed through a larger one during the preceding night. Sergeant Bollinger's alertness and Captain Troyan's language skills led to more interest in this strange source of information. Some tour officers gradually began to push the envelope by actively seeking areas where the Soviet military dumped their trash.

Based on John Fahey's account in his *Licensed to Spy*, we can conclude that in 1960-62, trash collection was not yet a well-developed operation. The one trip he reports that aimed at picking up debris from a Soviet training area bore no resemblance to the trash collection long underway by the 1970s. The implication that Operation SANDDUNE was simply a scouring of field latrines—heard by me also from other sources who had not served at USMLM—needs to be put to rest.

Up to the arrival of Colonel Peter Thorsen in 1974, trash collection was haphazard at best. Thorsen and Ground Operations Chief, Lieutenant Colonel Randall Greenwalt, quickly grasped the value of the materials Captain Troyan was bringing in. They instituted a more systematic program at USMLM. This included, according to the 1976 USMLM Unit History, "a heightened appreciation... for the intelligence value of trash; deliberate targeting of known dumps; an effort to identify other dumps, including coordination with air reconnaissance assets; and partial translation and terse analysis at USMLM to point the analyst in the right direction..."

Nick Troyan took me out on my first collection mission targeted on a trash dump. It was not a large deposit. Rather, it was an area in the woods just across the street from an installation that housed the 34th Guards Artillery Division, not far from the Potsdam House. The Soviets had discarded several training posters and notebooks. We loaded up what we could in the trunk of the car. Back at the operations center in Berlin, we translated enough to tell analysts at USAREUR and in Washington what we had collected.

In those days, we had not identified many trash dumps. But with Chief of USMLM's new emphasis on these targets, we began to search for them and mark them on our maps. I soon began working the trash dumps on my own. Nick and I hardly ever went on tour without looking for new trash dumps. If we found any we couldn't work at the time, we made note of their locations for future exploitation.

We were not likely to find operational battle plans for GSFG, but one never knew. Once I found a map with arrows showing Soviet units attacking Berlin. All Americans living in Berlin were well aware that in the event of a Soviet-initiated attack on NATO, we would almost instantly become casualties or prisoners. The possibility that I had found an attack plan on Berlin made my document urgent enough that I immediately returned to West Berlin. When I got back and was able to study the map more thoroughly, I realized that what I had "discovered" was a map depicting *The* Battle of Berlin by the Soviet Army in 1945. It was apparently part of a political or history class given to GSFG soldiers or officers. A sense of relief on my part was mixed with some embarrassment that I had not recognized the true nature of the document from the outset.

By the end of 1976, the USMLM Unit History reported approximately 40 percent of ground intelligence reports derived from SANDDUNE. Among Mission findings that year were a "technical maintenance manual for the T-62 tank" and "a notebook with complete characteristics and operating parameters" of a Soviet military radio station—something that was very valuable to the SIGINT community. Based on materials collected from trash dumps, the Mission was able to provide important information on "the staff of GSFG Headquarters, three army-level headquarters, three divisional headquarters and, in the case of one division, echelons down to and including battalion level."

The Chief of Mission changed in June 1977. Although there appears to have been an initial diminution in the emphasis on SANDDUNE for the last half of that year, by 1978, the project began to really bloom. As glowing evaluations started coming in from higher headquarters and national agencies, the unique value of this source of intelligence began to be appreciated by the new chief. USMLM began to devote more personnel and resources to the project. By the end of 1979, "almost half of all Intelligence Information Report (IIR) pages... contained translations of recovered documents." In 1981, SANDDUNE reports accounted for 47 percent of all USMLM IIRs evaluated as "of major significance." The 1983 Unit History reported SANDDUNE operations documented differences between wartime and peacetime manning of GSFG military units, findings that were of great value to NATO forces and to U.S. national war planning.

BRIXMIS also realized the value of documents obtained from trash dumps and developed their own systematic program, called "Operation Tomahawk." Steve Gibson, a former member of BRIXMIS, provides a detailed account of Operation Tomahawk in his *The Last Mission Behind the Iron Curtain*. Richard Aldrich, in his *the hidden hand*, writes that "rain-sodden notebooks and schedules of newly arrived materiel with sources and serial numbers for the latest equipment...were gold dust to the growing army of analysts in London and Washington."

Even during my years at the Mission (1976-77), there appeared to be more materials and reports than national agencies could handle. We heard through the grapevine that many of the items being sent to the Defense Intelligence Agency were just piling up in a room somewhere because there wasn't enough linguist support to process them. (A shortage of qualified linguists in intelligence continues to be a serious weak link in our military intelligence system.) As stated above, Nick and I performed cursory translations on the materials we were sending in, but we didn't have the time to do a thorough job on all that we collected.

Later, by 1979, national agencies put more resources into the project, and a special SANDDUNE section was set up at USMLM. Three U.S. civilians were hired and linguist support came by contract or periodic temporary duty from nine military units spread from Ft Richardson, Alaska; U.S. Army National Guard in Salt Lake City, Utah; Fort Bragg, North Carolina; Arlington Hall, Virginia; to Munich. Linguists from Teufelsberg made substantial contributions to the SANDDUNE Project. Student officers at USARI in Garmisch spent two weeks at a time at USMLM, working on the documents. Several of these officers would later serve at USMLM and become collectors of SANDDUNE materials themselves.

Many of the documents from SANDDUNE collection operations dealt with technical matters such as specifications and parameters for various artillery pieces, anti-aircraft systems, and vehicles. Others revealed training schedules; for example, the lesson plans "for an entire year for the ZSU-23-4 [anti-aircraft system] platoon of a tank regiment. The information included technical parameters of radar and armament, operating procedures, formations, and "Identification Friend or Foe" measures, and provided insights into tactical operations and capabilities of the ZSU-23-4 element of a tank regiment."

USMLM analysts used several documents as a basis for "conclusive" documentation on the ethnic makeup of GSFG forces. Germans, Jews, Lithuanians, Latvians, and Estonians, for example, were "as a matter of policy, not assigned to GSFG." Soviet authorities considered them to be of questionable loyalty, especially outside the USSR. Furthermore, almost all officers, warrant officers and NCOs were Russian, Ukrainian or Belorussian—the three Slavic nationalities in the Soviet Army.

SANDDUNE eventually became one of the most valuable sources of intelligence in USMLM's entire history. Likewise in the history of BRIXMIS. Geraghty reports a British intelligence officer flying to Berlin to personally tell a BRIXMIS officer that an item he had recovered from his trash dump operation—Operation Tomahawk—was "the most important thing we have had from any source for ten years."

I was amazed at the materials the Soviets discarded. Some documents even had classified markings. But even those simple items that contained lecture notes or commentary on fellow officers were useful to an intelligence community that had no other source to learn about everyday life in the Soviet Army. The value of the information we gleaned from these trash collection efforts sensitized me to the value of my own personal documents. I began to place personal and financial correspondence in "burn bags" that we kept in the office for incineration of classified documents. The lesson of the trash dumps remains with me to this day. Now, many years after retirement, I still burn personal and financial correspondence at my home.

Chapter 19
Deadman and Mud

After nearly a year of touring, I was now qualified to take new tour officers—back-seaters—on collection tours. I was thrilled to learn that my first back-seater would be a close friend. Major Rich Kosevich and I first met when we both taught Russian at West Point. Our wives and children became good friends during our time there. Rich and I, sometimes accompanied by our oldest children, had backpacked and climbed the Adirondack Mountains together in upstate New York. Rich was a West Point graduate, Class of 1963, and an armor officer of Serbian descent. He was the most conscientious officer I knew when it came to improving his Russian. He spoke much better Russian when our assignments were over at West Point than he did when we arrived three years earlier.

When he left the teaching assignment at West Point, Rich underwent the normal Foreign Area Officer training in Garmisch at USARI and arrived at USMLM on June 1, 1977. Later, after I left USMLM, Rich would become one of the Mission's primary interpreters. During Operation Cervine Twist (see Chapter 22), he played an important role as one of my key interpreters in Heidelberg.

Photo 23: Major Rich Kosevich and the author on tour.

Rich was anxious to get out into East Germany and "mix it up" with the Soviet Army. Staff Sergeant Ralph Germaine and I picked him up at his quarters around 6 a.m. This was a June morning and it was already daylight. My plan was to show Rich some installation coverage, search for military convoys and when all our tasks had been completed, to visit the pipe store in Erfurt. Rich also smoked a pipe and I wanted to show him this rare private business where he could buy some nice pipes for very little money. At the time, the exchange rate between the U.S. dollar and the East Mark was 10 to 1. (The West Mark exchanged at about 3 to 1.) We were dressed in our class A uniforms, complete with blouses (green jackets with all our insignia) and ties. Since we were going to be spending some of our time in the city of Erfurt, we wanted to be as presentable to the East German public as American officers should be. We were driving a new white Opel Diplomat instead of one of our olive drab Broncos or Opels.

As we crossed the Glienicke Bridge from West Berlin, I went through the same routine with Rich about surveillance that the experienced tour officer had done for me nearly a year earlier. We could see no narks waiting in ambush as we entered Potsdam. Perhaps they had taken off in pursuit of some other Allied Mission tour that crossed over earlier in the morning. By the time we reached the vicinity of the Potsdam House, however, we saw a Soviet-built white Moskvich with two narks waiting at the turn to Am Lehnitzsee, at the end of which was our compound. Rich picked up on them immediately.

"Yeah. Well at least we know where they are for now," I said. "We have to count on there always being some kind of surveillance, so it's good to identify it as soon as possible."

"We'll be able to outrun them, I'm sure," Rich said.

"Most of the time. If there aren't too many of them. Lots of times they're just pests. It depends on what we want to do and how well equipped they are."

When we left the Potsdam House with our *Kiste*, we took the Berlin Ring and headed south, traveling between 50 and 55 miles per hour. I hoped the slower speed would lull our surveillance into complacence and make it easier when the time came to lose them. At the first major interchange, I instructed Staff Sergeant Germaine to continue east on the Ring. Rich was looking at the map.

"Yasha, aren't we going south?"

"Eventually," I answered. "By passing up the E6 Autobahn, we can expect the narks to call ahead to alert their comrades that we're headed their way and possibly going toward Dresden or other points southeast."

"How'll we get back to our route? Turn off at the Beelitz intersection and find another way back to the Autobahn?"

"Exactly. But we have to lose the narks first. Go ahead, Ralph, open it up."

We had to rely on speed because we were traveling in broad daylight. No fancy manipulation of the vehicle lights would work here. The West German Opel was a two-wheel-drive vehicle and we quickly reached 100 miles per hour, fortunately, in light traffic. The Soviet Moskvich quickly fell back and was nowhere in sight at the point where we turned south toward Beelitz. When we reached town, we took another highway west that put us back on E6.

Going through Beelitz, we drove very carefully so as not to attract the attention of the VOPOS. If they sighted us and realized who we were, they would follow us to the end of town and then, possibly, alert other surveillance teams ahead. That would have defeated our just completed maneuver to evade the Potsdam narks. The only markings on our car that identified us as a Mission tour were the two license plates with the American flags and the number 23 painted on them. But being in a plain white sedan gave us some advantage.

Now we were clear of any more large towns, and we began to anticipate our collection mission. Our first stop would be an East German military facility that was situated in the middle of a field, surrounded by trees.

It was far from any population center or other military installation and was barely noticeable from the road. Our task was to try to determine what kind of unit it was. If we could get good photography of buildings, vehicles, and antennas, analysts back in Heidelberg or Washington, DC, would be able to identify the unit type.

Covering East German targets was more dangerous than covering Soviet targets. The East German population held no love for the Soviet Army or its occupation of their country. Often they would help out by telling us when and where Soviet convoy movements had taken place. When they recognized a Mission vehicle, they would often smile and give us the thumbs up. However, this was not the case when we were snooping around East German military facilities. The East German military (National Volksarmee—NVA) was also more aggressive than their Soviet military counterparts. The NVA resented their subservient status to, and dependence on, the Soviets. And they resented our right to travel around the GDR and spy on them, as well as on the Soviets. At every chance, the NVA would take out their frustration on Allied Missions. Some of the worst incidents involving vehicle rammings were perpetrated by the NVA. Several times the Soviets had to intercede for us with East German civil and military authorities.

The target installation was some distance from Potsdam. As we drove south, it began to rain hard. That slowed us down. One thing I didn't want was to get involved in an accident. I considered accidents in wartime to be the ultimate personal disaster. (Of course, we weren't engaged in a war in the normal sense, although we were already behind a potential "enemy's" front line.) To be killed by a sniper or a mine, even by friendly fire, was a natural hazard of war. But in a stupid accident that could have been avoided? I knew many soldiers had been killed in vehicle accidents in Vietnam, probably in all modern wars. General George Patton died as the result of an auto accident in Germany just after the end of World War II. I usually tried to keep our fast and seemingly reckless driving to a minimum and to use our speed only when I thought the operational situation called for it. There was no longer any need for speed today.

The rain had stopped by the time we reached the target area. The sun had come out, but there were puddles of standing water on the road. We saw only a few farmhouses and some cattle grazing. We found a grove of trees on a small hill near the road and pulled in there. All three of us got out of the vehicle and stretched our legs. Ralph retrieved a thermos of coffee, while Rich and I lit our pipes.

"We'll hide here for awhile to see if there's any reaction to our arrival in the area," I said to Rich.

"I can see some antennas in the installation from here," he noted. "I'll take a couple of photos from here with the telescopic lens." The antennas were visible just above the trees. I could see Rich was going to be a good tour officer; he would seize upon any opportunity to acquire information.

The only road into the installation was from the south, on the opposite side of the installation from where we were parked. There was no way we could use that road without being detected. That meant we would have to go across the open field and get into the forest that surrounded the installation.

"We can't sneak across an open field in the daytime," I said. "We'll have to make a dash for it and just hope no one sees us."

"I don't think they'll be able to see us from the German installation, given how thick the trees are. They might hear us though," Rich responded.

"Let's check out the ground. It rained pretty hard," I said.

The three of us walked around in the grove, testing the surface. I ventured out to the open area.

"Ralph, what do you think?"

"If it's no worse than this we'll have no problem, sir," he answered. "Especially if we get up enough speed." Ralph considered himself responsible for operation of the vehicle. In a way he was. He was an expert driver and I relied on him to give me the straight skinny on all possibilities and potential problems. But I would make the final decision about whether to go or not go. I took out the binoculars and surveyed the open field we would have to cross. There were some low spots, but there was also plenty of vegetation that should give us some traction.

"O.K. Let's mount up and give it a try," I said.

We moved slowly down the hill toward the side road we had come in on. At what looked like the shortest distance from the road to the tree line, I instructed Ralph to turn off and head for the woods.

"Give it all you got, Ralph."

The engine roared and we spun off the road across the field. We hadn't gone 150 feet when the ground softened and the car slowed, then stopped. We had become mired in mud. Rich and I jumped out and surveyed the situation. We were in a low area that still had some standing water in it. We walked forward and found firm ground about fifty feet ahead that appeared to continue all the way to the tree line. The ground behind us was likewise in good shape. I got back in the car.

"We're in a mud hole, but the ground ahead of us is not bad. We might be able to advance by pushing the car," I said. "Ralph, you stay at the wheel and Rich and I will push."

Rich and I removed our uniform blouses, loosened our ties, and rolled up our trousers. We were going to get muddy no matter what. With Rich pushing on the left rear and I on the right rear, Ralph attempted to advance the car slowly. The wheels spun and splattered mud on us and on the car, but we weren't having much success.

"We can use the deadman, sir," Ralph shouted out his window.

We stopped pushing for a few moments while I thought about our situation. If we could winch the car to the firm ground, we could reach the woods, do our thing, and hope the sun would dry the mud while we were in the forest. If we weren't detected by the East German military in the installation, we might even overnight in the forest. I opened the trunk and looked at the deadman gear—a heavy steel plate, a metal stake, and the winching apparatus. As I stood there about to make a decision, Ralph called out again from the front seat.

"Sir, look to the road. There's a vehicle coming by."

I looked and quickly recognized it as the kind of vehicle driven by German foresters. When it got to the point where we had left the road, it slowed and the driver looked our way, apparently trying to figure out why a shiny, but mud-splattered white sedan was stuck in the middle of the field. As an official in the East German government, he would know full well there was an NVA military unit in the middle of the forest. Therefore, we couldn't count on his willingness to look the other way. I saw no antennas on his vehicle, so assumed he had no radio. If he were going to report us to anyone, he would have to drive to the nearest police or military facility. The forester sped up and disappeared along the road.

"Now what?" asked Rich.

"We're going to have to move fast. Usually we can count on 15 minutes before someone shows up to further investigate," I said as I began removing the deadman and winch gear. "Here, Rich, help me get this set up. Ralph, get out and help us get hooked up. We're going to abort the mission and return to the road."

I placed the deadman about forty feet to the rear of the car and began to drive the stake through a hole in the middle. That would secure the deadman well enough that we could use it as an anchor to winch the car backward. Ralph hooked the steel cable to the rear of the car and the winch to the deadman. Then each of us took turns cranking the winch as fast as we could. At first the car hardly budged. After only a few minutes we began to slow down. It was obvious that our adrenalin was at a higher level than our physical strength.

Ralph cranked the longest of the three of us. Finally, the Opel slowly came back towards us through the mud. When we brought the car up to the deadman, we disconnected the winch and Ralph got back in. Rich and I pushed from the front. Ralph was getting some traction now and he carefully inched back across the deadman, making sure he didn't accelerate too fast and start the wheels spinning again.

"I think we can make it now," he said.

Rich and I rushed to the deadman, pulled the stake out and placed everything back in the trunk. We jumped in the car and slowly at first, then faster, traveled in reverse back to the road.

"Let's go back up to our hiding place in the grove of trees," I said. "We'll try to clean the car off before we get back on the road."

We drove up to our parking spot and got out to look the car over. The windows were splattered with mud and the side mirrors were completely caked over—not to mention the two American majors dressed in class A uniforms. We had mud up to the knees of our trousers and blotches of mud on our shirts.

"So much for our visit to the pipe shop," I said. "We can do that another time."

Suddenly, a woman came around the corner. When she saw us she stopped.

"Ach, mein Gott!" she exclaimed as she dropped the two pails of milk she was carrying, turned and ran back in the direction she had come from. Although this startled us also, after a few seconds of silence, we began to laugh. What in the world did she think she saw? How would she describe the scene to her family?

We took out a five-gallon jug of water from the trunk, cleaned the windows and mirrors, brushed as much mud from our uniforms as we could, and got back in the car.

"O.K. On to the next target," I said. "We can cover some of them from the car or find places where we can get out and still not scare the hell out of the German population."

We spent the rest of the day photographing Soviet installations, a couple of them near Erfurt. That night we selected an observation point near a railroad line where we could watch for shipments of military equipment. While Sergeant Germaine was catching a few Zs in preparation for his turn on watch, Rich and I stood out in the crisp night air, smoking our pipes and talking about our days at West Point.

"What a change this is from West Point," said Rich.

"Yeah. Would you've ever guessed then that someday we'd be here in the middle of East Germany 'spying' on the Soviets?" I asked.

"No," he answered. "This is almost surreal. But I love it." He looked at our uniforms and laughed. "I don't think we'd have been very presentable like this at West Point."

But mud-crusted uniforms were a small price to pay for evading capture by the East German military.

CHAPTER 20
WHY DIDN'T YOU RUN?

Getting clobbered was an inevitable hazard for Mission teams collecting intelligence in East Germany. Although clobbers were sometimes interesting, even exciting, they didn't present the officer involved with any sense of accomplishment. At the very least, clobbers diminished or prevented a tour's ability to accomplish its tasks.

We often tried to avoid detention by outrunning Soviet and East German pursuers. Getting clobbered often meant in one way or another we had gotten ourselves into a situation in which the only option was to allow the Soviets to detain us. In other words, it could be viewed as a failure on the part of a tour officer who had not planned correctly or who had let his guard down.

There were exceptions, of course. On my first and second clobbers—at the gas station in Wismar and our encounter with the "chain" gang on the bridge in Potsdam—there was little we could have done to avoid the detention. On the other hand, the clobber near Prenzlau, where the motorcyclist detained us, was clearly an instance where I failed to plan a reliable escape route.

The circumstances surrounding my fourth and final clobber were such that the incident might have gone both ways. That is, I had a choice whether to attempt an escape or to let the Soviets keep us boxed in.

Our assignment on that day was to patrol the Potsdam Local Area, an area within about a 25-mile radius of the city. The Allied Missions took turns conducting 24-hour tours in the Local Area. There were many Soviet military units and facilities there—several regiments of the 35th Motorized Rifle Division and the 10th Guards Tank Division, a self-propelled artillery regiment, a surface-to-air missile brigade, and the 34th Artillery Division (very close to the Potsdam House). Generally, if we hadn't been given any specific targets, we'd simply patrol the area monitoring local activity or looking for targets of opportunity.

I recall such a target of opportunity that had appeared during an earlier Potsdam local tour. One late afternoon, my driver and I came upon the 35th Motorized Rifle Division training area, which was to the south of the highway. We slowed down. I saw what looked to be new tanks on the firing range. Looking through my binoculars, I saw T-64 tanks, recently introduced into GSFG. So far, the Mission had no ground photography of this tank in the open.

"Pull over," I said to my driver.

I took out my 1000mm lens, attached it to the camera and pushed the button for automatic film advance. Individuals and small groups of soldiers were walking along the road past the car. They paid no attention to us, possibly because our Bronco resembled the Soviet UAZ-469 jeep.

"Keep the motor running," I instructed the driver. "We may have to leave in a hurry."

I rolled the window down and rested the lens on the doorframe. A 1000mm lens has a high magnification factor, so it requires a lot of light and a relatively slow shutter speed. Since the daylight was beginning to fade, I opened the aperture as far as possible. To counter the vibration of our running car, I set the speed slightly higher than normal and began to shoot several frames of a T-64. As I peered through the viewfinder, however, I saw only a small portion of the tank filled the entire lens. I began adjusting the focus and moving the lens back and forth around the tank, hoping to get enough good shots to put together a collage when we returned to Berlin. Just then, someone yelled at us in Russian.

"Go," I barked to the driver, as I pulled the lens back inside the car. "We've got all we're going to get this time." As we sped away, we could see in our rearview mirror several Soviet soldiers running toward us. Then they stopped and pointed in our direction, as if they were telling someone "They went that-a-way." No vehicle, however, took out after us in pursuit.

When the roll of film was later developed, sure enough, only a few frames were in focus. They provided analysts some information but it would take more photography to give them a good technical picture of this new Soviet tank. Other tour officers and a special air reconnaissance project soon filled in the gaps.

Now here we were, touring the Potsdam Local Area again. We had been on patrol since early morning and had seen nothing remarkable so far. We decided to turn off into what we knew was a small local training area. In doing so, we passed an MRS without batting an eye. As I mentioned earlier, the MRSs were erected locally and all the Allied Missions ignored them. On this late-August day the ground was firm and we could navigate just about any terrain, which made it likely we could outrun and outmaneuver just about any form of detention attempt. We were, however, limited by the fact that there were only so many places we could run to in the Local Area. We wouldn't be able to get across the Glienicke Bridge with Soviets of MfS in pursuit because of the barriers on the bridge. If we ran to the Potsdam House, there would surely be someone waiting for us before we could get into the compound.

Finding nothing in the training area, we decided to return to the main road. Just as we left the dirt road (out from behind the MRS) we saw a canopied Soviet 2 1/2-ton truck moving along the main road. The truck slowed, pulled off the highway in our direction and stopped, almost blocking our access to the highway.

"What're you doing? Get the hell out of the way," I said aloud, as if talking to the Soviet truck driver.

"No problem, sir. I can go around it," my driver said.

I was about to nod my head in consent, when, suddenly, soldiers jumped out of the back of the truck and quickly surrounded us. Altogether there were about forty of them. A lieutenant jumped down from the passenger's seat of the truck. None of the soldiers was armed, but they formed a ring around us and effectively boxed us in from all directions.

"I can get out of this, sir," my sergeant said.

"But look," I said, "they're standing too close together."

"They'll move when I start toward them, by God."

"No," I said quickly. "No. Someone could get hurt."

I had briefed all my drivers that when we got into tight situations, they were to tell me quickly 1) whether they believed we could get away, 2) couldn't get away, or 3) if they weren't sure one way or the other. I would then decide what to do. This situation today was one from which we might be able to escape. I didn't hesitate at the time to make the decision not to run, although later I would be challenged on whether it was the right one. It just didn't seem worth it to risk someone getting injured or killed.

At first, no one approached our vehicle. The lieutenant stayed with his soldiers. A Soviet UAZ-469 jeep, going by on the highway, stopped, turned around, and pulled up beside the truck. Two captains got out. After a few words with the lieutenant, they walked toward us. Once they reached us, one captain signaled for me to roll my window down. I cracked it slightly.

"What are you doing here," asked one of the officers.

"Nothing. Just driving around," I answered. "Do you know who we are?"

"You're Americans. From the Military Liaison Mission. It says so on your license plate."

"Are you from the *komendatura*?" I asked.

"No. We were just driving by and saw the commotion." By this time the lieutenant had walked over and joined the two captains.

"I've called the *komendatura*," he said to the other officers. "Someone should be here soon."

The Soviet officers began to engage me in conversation. This time it was about politics in the United States. During our discussion, I denied that wealthy industrialists controlled American political leaders. I fended off questions about whether I agreed with various U.S. foreign policies, explaining that as a soldier it was not my place to criticize or otherwise comment publicly on U.S. policies. I said American soldiers have a right to their own opinions, but they keep them to themselves. We don't play an active role in American political life. We just vote, which is a personal matter for each soldier. They thought that was strange and told me all Soviet officers were political. They were even required to participate actively in Communist Party affairs. I could see I would have a difficult time explaining to them what being politically active means in a multiparty state.

I was experienced enough now with detentions not to get too worked up. I was sure we had exited from behind the MRS before anyone in the truck saw us. We had been stopped in an open area. We had no specific targets to work on that day. We had no deadlines. I was content just to wait for the *komendatura* representative, and then I would complain to him about being illegally detained.

The conversation continued about America—salaries, houses, cars and so forth. The time passed rather quickly. No one came from the *komendatura*. I took advantage of the opportunity to show the Soviet officers a photo of me talking with General Ivanovsky, their CINC.

"Yes, I know General Ivanovsky," I said in response to their questions. "He and I have worked together on several occasions."

There had been cases where a tour officer, when detained by the Soviets, stated he was "a member of the Soviet Forces." This was patently untrue. Although lying to the Soviets was one thing, and was usually acceptable, this kind of lie could have caused severe repercussions if the Soviets had decided to charge the Mission officer with impersonating a Soviet officer. I found that simply showing the photo and stating the truth—that General Ivanovsky and I had met on several occasions—was sufficient to temper any inclination on the part of the detaining officers to commit some belligerent act.

The lieutenant went back to the jeep a couple of times, apparently to call his *komendatura*. Finally, after about 45 minutes, he came back, whispered to the captains, and told me we were free to go. He ordered the soldiers to make way for us. They stood back and watched us as we pulled onto the main road and turned toward Potsdam, rather than toward Berlin. We decided to continue our patrolling for the rest of the day.

When I returned to Berlin the next day, I made my usual routine report. A couple of days later, the new Chief of USMLM came to my office carrying a copy of my report.

"Tell me again what happened on this clobber," he said.

"Well, it's just like I reported it, sir. We got surrounded by a truckload of Sovs."

"You didn't try to run?"

"No, sir. It would've been too risky. The soldiers were almost shoulder to shoulder."

"So you didn't even try?"

"Not really. The driver thought we could get away, but I decided that would have been too dangerous."

"I see," said the chief. He looked over my report slowly.

"I think you should've run."

I didn't say anything. The colonel turned and left.

I was satisfied with my decision not to run. There was no need to show off for the Soviets. They knew already what our cars and drivers were capable of. Furthermore, I was carrying no material of immediate intelligence value. Even if the Soviets had broken into our vehicle they would have found little but food, maps, and photography equipment. Most of all, I thought the chance of someone getting injured, or worse, was pretty high. In short, there was no justifiable intelligence need to break out of the circle of Soviet soldiers.

The fact that we weren't taken to the *komendatura* was enough proof to me that the Soviets didn't think we had done anything wrong, so it wasn't worth their time to bring us in and then later have to fill out all manner of reports. Or maybe my photo with General Ivanovsky had some effect on their zeal to have me detained. The lieutenant had taken it upon himself to use his soldiers to detain us, but the lieutenant's decision apparently was overridden by his *komendatura*. I was reminded of the overzealous lieutenant during my first clobber in Wismar.

That summer of 1977 was very eventful. The first couple of months I had been busy with Operation Cervine Twist (See Chapter 22). In June, we changed chiefs at the Mission. Our departing chief, Colonel Thorsen, was an old Russian hand. He had served as an attaché in Moscow and Warsaw and knew how to intimidate or cajole the Russians at will. He had a sixth sense about how far to push the Russians before their reactions would make his efforts counterproductive.

The new chief, Colonel Don Stovall, had served earlier as a tour officer (1969-71). Mission tour officers were sometimes so aggressive during those years that the Soviets and some staff members at our headquarters in Heidelberg referred to them as "cowboys." They were inclined to drive fast and reckless, sometimes endangering civilians on sidewalks and in small villages. Colonel Stovall returned to a Mission that had changed considerably.

Lieutenant Colonel Randall Greenwalt, our Ground Team Chief, who had also served at USMLM during an earlier era and who would later become Chief of the Mission, recognized these changes immediately. After a year of duty under Colonel Thorsen, he wrote in the 1976 Unit History:

> The intelligence collection atmosphere has decidedly improved. Previous "escape and evade" tactics which often led to exciting, but pointless, high-speed chases and concerted efforts to detain tours, have been replaced by a more subdued, stealthful style of collection and *a preparedness to accept detention, rather than escalate a situation.* [Italics added] (USMLM Unit History, 1976)

Colonel Thorsen's philosophy was that tour officers should behave like professionals, be aggressive in our collection efforts, but never risk our own lives or those of the Soviets or the East German public. In his introduction to the 1975 USMLM Unit History, he wrote: "We must continue to be aware of political implications in all that we do... Inherent frustration is a thing we must live with, remembering that there will always be another day."

When we made Colonel Thorsen's farewell call at Headquarters, GSFG, Colonel General Grinkevich, Chief of Staff of GSFG, told my colonel: "We respect you, Colonel Thorsen, for the way you and your officers have conducted themselves since you took over the Mission. Not like the old 'cowboy' days." Grinkevich smiled and added, "And I bet your intelligence production increased manyfold over that of the earlier chiefs."

My fourth clobber never made it into the 1977 USMLM Unit History, perhaps because it never escalated into a trip to the Potsdam *komendatura*. But I often wondered if the reason for its omission was that the new chief didn't think it should have occurred in the first place.

PART IV: INTERPRETING AND DEPARTURE

Chapter 21
Interpreting

Despite our emphasis on intelligence collection, liaison occasionally took on great importance. The Mission was still the conduit between various American headquarters in West Germany and HQ GSFG in Wünsdorf, East Germany. Over the years, the Mission had been an indispensable vehicle for the commanders-in-chief to resolve several conflicts. It had also served as a venue for get-togethers on a more informal basis between the senior officers of each headquarters.

When there was a meeting between American and Soviet military officials, the role of the interpreter was critical. For Mission interpreters, the frequent meetings at the Soviet liaison office, SERB, provided good practice for more important events. When I arrived at USMLM, Captain Nick Troyan, bilingual in English and Russian, served as the primary interpreter. He had been at the Mission since February 1974, but was due to rotate out for another assignment in the next few months. He and I began sharing interpreter chores as I prepared to become his replacement the following spring. After doing an apprenticeship under Captain Troyan, on 14 August 1976, the day came for my first "solo."

"So, Yasha, you're going with Thorsen to SERB? Is this your first trip as an official interpreter?" Nick asked as he pulled me aside just before I left the office on that solo trip.

"Yeah, the Chief's going to meet with Colonel Porvatov."

"Let me tell you something about how to handle Lieutenant Yegorov, the SERB interpreter. You've already met him. Just remember, the first thing you need to do when you share interpreting with him is put him in his place. His English isn't as good as our Russian, so the first time he makes a mistake, jump in and correct him."

"Wouldn't that embarrass him in front of his boss?"

"Of course. But that's not our concern. What's important is for him to know you're monitoring him all the time."

Up to now, I had only limited interpreting experience—twice in Vietnam during interrogation of North Vietnamese officers and once at the Soviet Military Liaison Mission in Frankfurt when I was assigned to Heidelberg. Nick had served at the Mission for over two years already. His willingness to take me under his wing gave me a running start about some of the ins and outs of interpreting at USMLM.

I was nervous, of course, about this first meeting at SERB. One of the problems in such meetings is that you never know ahead of time what's going to be said. Colonel Thorsen could tell I was a little tense.

"Your first trip to SERB, eh?" he asked.

"Yes, sir."

Photo 24: Captain Nick Troyan greets General Blanchard. To Blanchard's right is Colonel Peter Thorsen; to his left is Lieutenant Colonel Randall Greenwalt.

"Well, Nick tells me you speak better Russian than he does, so I'm sure you don't have to worry about anything."

"What do you think the meeting will be about, sir?"

"Oh, I imagine some bullshit about one of our tours that was shot at on the 11th. The Sovs may try to preempt our protest."

"Sounds pretty chicken shit," I commented.

"It doesn't matter. It'll be a trumped-up charge," Colonel Thorsen said. "Maybe it'll be a protest about an earlier SMLM-F detention near Oberdachstetten in West Germany. The Soviet Mission violated a PRA. Our MPs had every right to detain them."

"Soviet 'reciprocity,' I suppose."

"You don't know the Sovs yet," he added. "Reciprocity's a big thing for them. And they get away with it too. I wish our own people would use a little more reciprocity against the Sovs sometimes."

Looking back now, I recall how reciprocity was always a touchy subject with anyone who dealt with the Soviets on an official basis. For example, when the United States expelled a Soviet diplomat, usually with just cause, the USSR was quick to reciprocate by expelling a U.S. diplomat on manufactured grounds. But, when the Soviets committed some unjustifiable act against Westerners, there was often no immediate response on our part. The British tell of one case where the clearly unjustified expulsion of an officer from BRIXMIS resulted in such a delayed response from the British government, that when a member of SOXMIS was finally expelled three months later, the Soviets had apparently forgotten about the original incident and immediately expelled another BRIXMIS officer. As the author in *The Story of BRIXMIS 1946-1990* writes, "the Soviets certainly won that round by the score of 2 to 1."

As it turned out, I had no trouble with my first official interpreting assignment at SERB. Most of the time we listened to Colonel Porvatov's protest about the Soviet Mission detention in West Germany. Lieutenant Yegorov did most of the interpreting. Although he did make a couple of slips now and then, it didn't change anything substantive, so I kept my mouth shut. Colonel Thorsen didn't argue with Colonel Porvatov. He simply stated he would bring the protest to the attention of higher headquarters. I got the distinct impression both sides were simply going through a *pro forma* exercise. The Chief of SERB said nothing about the USMLM tour being shot at. Colonel Thorsen didn't mention it because he had to await the official protest statement from Heidelberg.

During a subsequent meeting, Colonel Thorsen's actions taught me a useful lesson. On this occasion, we were doing the protesting. A SMLM-F team had, once again, entered an American PRA and photographed a U.S. military training exercise. After some initial chitchat, Colonel Thorsen launched into the protest. He raised his voice, slammed his fist on the table, and pointed out how USMLM teams always respect the Soviet PRAs in East Germany. I interpreted his remarks in a neutral tone. The Soviets sat quietly and listened to the chief. They were clearly cowed by the Chief's manner. The colonel was a big man and even though he delivered the protest in English, once they knew the context, they understood his point quite well even without me.

When Thorsen completed the protest, he sat back in his chair as if to let it all sink in. Then he reached into his pocket, pulled out a pack of cigarettes, took a cigarette and lit it.

"Colonel Porvatov, would you like one?" he said in a friendly manner as he passed the package across the table. "Lieutenant Yegorov, you too."

I interpreted my colonel's remarks while the Soviets just sat there dumbfounded. Lieutenant Yegorov looked at his colonel. The relief on the Soviet side was palpable. Colonel Porvatov then smiled and reached for the package.

"*Da. Spasibo.* Thank you," he said meekly. He took out a cigarette and passed the package to Lieutenant Yegorov.

"They say we're going to get a lot of snow this winter," said Colonel Thorsen.

"Yes... I've heard. But we Russians are used to snow."

The conversation continued about the weather. The two colonels were again involved in normal chitchat. But the way Colonel Thorsen handled the Soviets stuck in my mind.

On the way back to Berlin, I mentioned to the chief how the Soviets apparently had been intimidated by his delivery of the protest and then flustered when he offered them the cigarettes. Colonel Thorsen laughed.

"You gotta keep them off-balance, Major. Try never to let them know what your frame of mind is or what you're going to do next."

"But can't that lead to miscalculation?" I asked.

"Oh, we're not talking about high-level politics here. I mean this is the kind of thing you should do when you're dealing with them on a personal basis."

"I guess that would be a good idea on the road, on tour, also."

"Exactly. Make them work for their money."

As I gained more interpreting experience and Nick's time for departure grew nearer, I found myself involved in almost as many "liaison functions" as intelligence collection tours. In addition to the meetings at SERB, not all of which were confrontations, we had several social functions.

Social functions at Potsdam House in 1976-77 included Fourth of July and Labor Day picnics, and Thanksgiving dinners. Often, especially for the Fourth of July picnic, the Soviet officers would bring their families to Potsdam House. They may have wanted to make sure there were sufficient Soviet witnesses to the annual volleyball game between the Americans and Soviets, a game the Soviets always won. Little wonder, since most of the Soviet players were well over six feet tall. I'm sure they were specially assembled for the occasion.

A very special event took place each April, so long as there were no ongoing U.S.-Soviet crises. USMLM officers, NCOs and their families would join with the Soviets at the Potsdam House to celebrate the meeting in 1945 of our respective World War II armies on the banks of the Elbe River near Torgau. The USMLM Association website describes that historic event:

> On 25 April 1945, a unit of the 69th U.S. Infantry Division encountered Soviet soldiers. The battalion commander... crossed the Elbe River and was met by a Soviet major and two other soldiers. Later that afternoon, another U.S. patrol met Soviet troops on the girders of a twisted bridge over the Elbe.

A monument commemorating that meeting stands today in Torgau. (One of the two signatories of the Huebner-Malinin Agreement—at the time, Major General Clarence Huebner—commanded the U.S. V Corps to which the 69th Infantry was assigned. Shortly after the linkup, General Huebner met with his counterpart, Red Army XXXIV Corps commander, Lieutenant General Gleb Baklanov.)

Photo 25: The Torgau Monument. The inscription reads: "Glory to the victorious Red Army and the valiant troops of our Allies in the victory over Fascist Germany."

I served as the primary interpreter during the 1976 Thanksgiving Dinner at the Potsdam House. It was a large, gala affair, almost always attended by several Soviet generals and officers with their ladies.

At this dinner, the senior Soviet general present was Colonel General Grinkevich. Grinkevich was a professional chief of staff—the second most important officer in a Soviet military headquarters. He had served in that capacity at all echelons up to the current Group level. (He would later serve as Chief of Staff at the Headquarters, Soviet Ground Forces in Moscow, when

General Ivanovsky was CINC, Ground Forces.) When Grinkevich was the senior Soviet officer present, he was an imposing person—gregarious, outspoken, and jovial. He appeared quite relaxed with us Americans, but was very domineering, even imperious, with his own officers.

The official 1976 USMLM History reports that for the Thanksgiving Dinner: "Colonel General Grinkevich contributed greatly to this atmosphere as he related numerous amusing stories." One of his "amusing stories" was an off-color joke. I sat next to USAREUR Chief of Staff, Major General Groves, and interpreted the conversation between the two senior officers. Others at the table were having their own conversations, using both Soviet and U.S. Mission officers as interpreters. General Grinkevich decided to tell a chief-of-staff joke.

"You know, general," he began, as he addressed General Groves, "we chiefs of staff have the toughest job in the army."

When this was interpreted to General Groves, he smiled and nodded.

"I'll give you an example," continued General Grinkevich. "Two chiefs of staff were discussing the sex exploits of one commander. The first chief of staff asked, 'What do you think? Is having sex hard work or fun?' The second chief responded, 'Obviously, it's fun. If it were hard work, the commander would tell us to do it.'"

General Groves chuckled. He then turned to me and informed me that he would like to tell an off-color joke too. He told a joke about playing tennis without balls, using the double entendre of the word "balls."

All of a sudden I was stuck. The slang for testicles in Russian is *yaitsa*, 'eggs.' So what significance can there be of playing tennis without eggs? I looked over at

General Grinkevich and quickly explained the quandary caused by the two terms. I asked him to laugh after I said "tennis without eggs." He nodded his head and laughed appropriately at the end of the joke. Mrs. Thorsen was seated at the end of the long table between the two chiefs of staff. What she thought of General Groves' joke I couldn't tell. Fortunately, she didn't understand Russian, so she had no idea what I was telling General Grinkevich.

Frequently my experiences with the Soviet generals were not as an interpreter. We would have conversations of our own. My Russian appeared to place them more at ease and to bridge some psychological barrier. During informal conversations we were able to establish a form of casual rapport.

Photo 26: **The author interpreting Colonel Thorsen's remarks at the Thanksgiving Party, 1976. To my right is Major General Groves. In the lower right-hand corner of the picture is Colonel General Grinkevich. The dark-haired Soviet officer seated by the window behind me is Lieutenant Colonel Igor Kanavin, Chief of SERB.**

One example of this attitude toward me on the part of some of the Soviet generals began during Colonel Thorsen's farewell visit to the Soviet headquarters in Wünsdorf. Part of the farewell ceremony was an exchange of gifts. When the colonel and General Grinkevich had finished exchanging gifts, the general turned to me.

"You smoke a pipe, don't you, Major Holbrook?" I noted his use of my rank with some satisfaction.

"Yes, sir. I do."

"Have you ever smoked Soviet tobacco?"

"Yes, sir."

"What did you think of it?"

"I wasn't particularly crazy about it," I answered meekly. Colonel Thorsen frowned at me.

"I'm going to give you some premium Soviet tobacco. You'll like it. And you won't have to go home from this visit empty-handed."

I immediately recalled my experience during the trip Dex Dickinson and I had taken to the USSR in 1971 and my dislike of the tobacco I found there.

"No, sir. That's not necessary."

"Nonsense. You need to try some 'real' tobacco."

General Grinkevich pressed a button at his desk. In a few seconds a Soviet warrant officer entered the room.

"Go get a package of *"Zolotoye runo*," he ordered the warrant officer. "I want to give it to this American pipe smoker."

"Zolotoye runo" was Russian for "Golden Fleece'"—the best pipe tobacco the Soviets produced. The general and colonel resumed their conversation while I interpreted. In a few minutes, the warrant officer returned with a new pack of the pipe tobacco. The general handed it to me and said "Smoke it in good health. In good health, ha-ha."

That's not the end of the story, however. Several weeks later, I met General Grinkevich again, this time at the Potsdam House.

"Well, Major Holbrook, how did you like *Zolotoye runo?*"

I had to think fast. "Fine, General Grinkevich. I found a way to make it very tasty."

"How's that?"

"I mixed nine-tenths Virginia tobacco with one-tenth *Zolotoye runo*. The result was excellent."

Photo 27: Tobacco box top Colonel General Grinkevich gave me in Wünsdorf.

General Grinkevich looked at me for a moment and then burst out laughing. "That's what I like about you Americans," he said. "You're always direct."

On still another occasion, at the Potsdam House during a social function, I addressed Major General Vorobiov, Chief of GSFG Intelligence, as "Comrade General."

"We're not comrades," he said with a puzzled look.

"Yes, we are," I answered.

"How do you explain that?"

"You're an intelligence officer and I'm an intelligence officer. That makes us 'comrades by profession.'"

I was playing on the Russian way of expressing "mate." A classmate, roommate, teammate, or anyone of the same category or profession is expressed in Russian as *tovarisch po...*(comrade by/in...). General Vorobiov first scowled, then smiled and said, "Yes, I guess you're right then."

"And another thing, Comrade General. You look very much like my grandfather who emigrated from Lithuania when he was a boy."

"I'm too young to be your grandfather," quickly retorted General Vorobiov.

"Of course. I meant to say you look like my grandfather looked when he was young."

Photo 28: The author interpreting for Major General Groves and my grandfather-look-alike, Soviet Major General Vorobiov. At far left is George Gricius, a USMLM civilian.

The fact that Soviet generals sometimes related to me as if I were a junior colleague, rather than just an unidentified interpreter, I found particularly remarkable. I knew the Soviets often viewed interpreters as nonentities, sometimes taking them out of photos in Soviet newspapers, photos that occasionally maintained the interpreter's shadow!

Once, during the event I describe in the next chapter—Operation Cervine Twist—the Soviets were shown a wide array of combat demonstrations, including a demonstration firing by an artillery unit. When the artillery piece went off, I jumped. General Ivanovsky laughed, put his arm around my shoulder, and said, "You can always tell these intelligence types. They're not used to artillery fire."

Interpreting is a crucial and intense operation. Two people face each other and wish to communicate, but neither knows the other's language. Although oral interpretation is by its nature less exact than written translation, the quality of the interpretation can be enhanced by applying several measures. (Knowledge of the two languages is a given here. This may seem too obvious to mention, but lack of knowledge of one of the languages is often at the core of poor interpretation.)

One of the essential aspects of successful interpreting is the planning that goes (or should go) into the upcoming event. In the past, some high-level leaders have ignored the importance of interpreter planning. President Ford is reported to have gone behind closed doors with Soviet leader Brezhnev at their November 1974 summit in Vladivostok with no American interpreter whatsoever, thus relying only on the Soviet interpreter. Ford and Brezhnev were discussing limitations on our respective arsenals of nuclear arms. We may never know exactly what they said to each other.

President Carter failed to provide Steven Seymour with an advance copy of remarks he was planning to make at the Okecie International Airport in Warsaw in December 1977. After standing in freezing rain for hours awaiting the president, Seymour reportedly translated several of President Carter's comments in such a way that it caused all-around embarrassment for the Polish people and the U.S. presidential party. As the new ambassador in Moscow in 1943, Admiral Standley went to his first meeting with Stalin without an interpreter!

There were also some notable weaknesses in the way interpreting was handled at times at the Mission. In 1972, the USAREUR Chief of Staff met with his GSFG counterpart with only a Soviet interpreter present. Some USMLM chiefs were notorious for going to meetings at SERB without an interpreter. I know of no Chief of Mission, with the exception of Colonel Roland LaJoie— Chief, USMLM in 1983-86—who could speak Russian well enough to be sure he had caught everything the Soviets said.

Even if one did understand Russian well, my view was (and remains) that any time official business is conducted, the American representative should speak English and have an interpreter present—if only to confirm that such and such was said and/or decided upon. I resolved that, even though I spoke fluent Russian, if I were ever in a leadership position and required to discuss official business with the Soviets, I would speak English and have another American speaker of Russian present. The one time I found myself the sole American officer representing USMLM—at a border crossing by CINC GSFG—my conversation (in Russian) consisted of simple pleasantries. In that case, there was nothing for me to do but welcome the Soviet general to the U.S. Zone crossing point.

By 1976, I had spent 15 years studying Russian. I knew the language about as well as any non-native could. And I had a good grasp of the Russian history and culture, as well as Soviet politics. My interpreting experience at USMLM to date, however, had shown me I needed additional skills besides knowing the language. First of all, I needed more knowledge of the subject matter. I had to work hard, much of it "on-the-job-training," to master the terminology and specifications for Soviet military equipment.

I never reached what I considered a satisfactory level of understanding when it came to military technical subjects. Second, I had to learn to discern and translate quickly the true meaning and connotations of what was being said by both parties. Literal translation seldom did the job. Finally, for official protests and statements, I needed to find out what the original text was as much beforehand as possible. There was no room for error in an official statement. Fortunately, official statements were usually written down beforehand, even if delivered orally, so I could usually get a look at them before any meeting.

CHAPTER 22
OPERATION "CERVINE TWIST"

The most important interpreting event I was involved in at USMLM was the visit to CINC USAREUR, General (four-star) George Blanchard by CINC GSFG, Army-General (four-star equivalent) Evgenii Ivanovsky in July 1977.

Meetings between the commanders of the U.S. and Soviet armies in divided Germany dated back to the end of World War II. General Eisenhower met with Soviet Marshal Zhukov in Berlin in 1945. In the early 1950s, U.S. General Hoges and Soviet General Grechko exchanged visits to their respective headquarters. In 1962, Soviet Army-General Yakubovsky visited U.S. General Freeman in Heidelberg.

The mutual suspicion, as well as the actions and reactions on the part of USSR and the West that evolved into the Cold War, gradually began to dominate relations between the commanders of the American and Soviet armies in Germany. American commanders, however, continued to work to keep the lines of communications between the two headquarters on a rational basis. In 1966, CINC USAREUR, General James Polk, went to great pains to arrange a meeting with CINC GSFG, General Koshevoy. In June he began sending informal feelers to the Soviets through USMLM that he would like to meet with Koshevoy for lunch at the Potsdam House, as an initial step toward more comprehensive meetings between the two CINCs at their respective headquarters. After a formal invitation was extended to Koshevoy, it appeared for a while a meeting would take place. At the last minute, however, SERB informed the Chief of USMLM, that Koshevoy would not be able to attend the luncheon, due to the "press of business."

It was not until 1973 that the first CINC-CINC meeting of the modern Cold War era took place. U.S. General Michael Davison accepted an invitation from CINC GSFG, General Ivanovsky, to visit the Soviet headquarters in Wünsdorf. That visit became an important event for then Lieutenant General Blanchard, who at the time was the U.S. senior corps commander in Germany and a member of General Davison's entourage.

In 1986, I interviewed General Blanchard about the 1973 visit. According to him, everything the Soviets showed the Americans was fake. When the visitors entered the Soviet installation, the streets were uninhabited— no children in the playgrounds, no family members or soldiers walking around. The American visitors went first to a Soviet barracks. There they found the bayonets still covered in Cosmoline and the overcoats hanging in the closets smelled of mothballs. All the bunks in the barracks were decorated with knit coverlets and there were small rugs beside each soldier's bed. The Americans were told to look out the window to see Soviet soldiers doing physical training. What they saw was a troupe of acrobats, dressed in military uniforms, performing all sorts of gymnastic feats on swings and parallel bars in an athletic field. Later, in the mess hall, the Soviets showed the Americans a special table that was set aside for "birthday boys." The mess hall food was varied and exciting and included a variety of fresh vegetables and fruits. Everything throughout the visit seemed to General Blanchard and the others to be specially staged for the visitors.

The 1973 visit made such a negative impression on General Blanchard he resolved that if he ever had anything to do with a visit by the Soviet CINC to West Germany, he was determined to do just the reverse—to show the Soviets something realistic. General Blanchard would soon get his chance.

Plans for a return visit by General Ivanovsky to General Davison started in earnest in 1974, but President Nixon's resignation upset the apple cart and the visit was postponed. In 1975, General Blanchard became CINC USAREUR. Now he was in charge of planning for the Soviet general's visit.

As planners in Heidelberg were drawing up a concept of operations, they called upon the Mission for special expert advice. Colonel Thorsen sent Lieutenant Colonel Randall Greenwalt to brief the planning team in Heidelberg on the importance of showing the Soviets a U.S. Army in Europe that had essentially come out of the post-Vietnam doldrums. Greenwalt had been a tank battalion commander in Europe for two years. He saw firsthand how the army had turned around now that it was once again getting resources and qualified personnel previously allocated to the Vietnam War effort. His recommendations coincided perfectly with the overall concept General Blanchard had given his staff. Heidelberg named the plan "Operation Cervine Twist." (Whence that particular name—a word relating to deer—I don't know. The Army had a practice of sometimes using random and esoteric code words.) General Blanchard added one more stipulation to the operation: Cervine Twist must have comprehensive interpreter support.

I was put in charge of interpreting. USAREUR and USMLM decided that I should have as much contact with General Ivanovsky as possible. I met General Ivanovsky for the first time in April 1977, at the annual Torgau party at the Potsdam House. Nick Troyan was the primary interpreter, but I was able to quietly observe the Soviet CINC. I noted his confidence and diplomatic nature when talking about potentially controversial military issues. He was amiable, but he completely dominated the Soviet side of any conversation. (Even General Grinkevich kept his own counsel.) General Ivanovsky spoke intelligently, used good Russian, and apparently felt at ease in socializing with American officers. Both he and General Blanchard were old soldiers, veterans of World War II. Blanchard had been an enlisted artilleryman before he entered West Point, from which he graduated in 1944. Ivanovsky had been a tank company commander in the Battle of Berlin in 1945. Now they were both four-star generals, commanding armies that were poised to fight each other in the event of war.

In early June 1977, General Ivanovsky made a trip to Baden-Baden, West Germany, where the French military headquarters was located. His route necessitated a transit of the American Zone of West Germany. I was designated as the official U.S. representative at the Wartha crossing point on the Intra-German border into the American Zone. (Usually the Chief of USMLM carried out this ceremony.) I had my driver take a picture of Ivanovsky and me talking, a picture I carried with me for the rest of my time at USMLM. I used it once (see Chapter 20), when I was detained by the Soviets, to give them the impression Ivanovsky and I were on close terms.

Photo 29: The author greets Soviet Army-General Ivanovsky as the latter prepares to cross the border and transit the American Zone of West Germany.

My next meeting with Ivanovsky occurred on 21 June when the new Chief of USMLM, Colonel Don Stovall, traveled to Wünsdorf to present his letter of appointment to the Soviet CINC. I served as his interpreter on that trip.

At the beginning of July, I traveled to Heidelberg to help prepare General Blanchard for the visit and to arrange for other interpreters at the sites Ivanovsky would visit. Before I departed for West Germany, I called Senior Lieutenant Yegorov, the Soviet interpreter from SERB who would accompany General Ivanovsky. I asked to meet him at the Soviet officers' club in Potsdam. U.S. Lieutenant Berner and I met Yegorov there, and over lunch we worked out how we would handle the conversations of the two CINCs. During routine discussions, Yegorov would interpret from English to Russian and I would go from Russian to English. During toasts or speeches, he would translate Ivanovsky's remarks into English, while I would translate General Blanchard's speeches into Russian.

When I reported to General Blanchard in Heidelberg, he assigned me a space in his large office, where I worked on translating menus and briefings. General Blanchard conducted his normal business with various staff officers, while I sat there, listened, and studied my general. The CINC told me he wanted us to get to know each other well enough that when the visit occurred we would have full confidence in each other, and he could rely on my judgment about the intricacies of dealing with Ivanovsky and his generals.

During lulls in General Blanchard's work, I would brief the CINC on various aspects of the Soviet Army, or go over biographic information on the Soviet visitors, or articles General Ivanovsky had published in Soviet magazines and newspapers. I gave General Blanchard some highlights from the new Soviet Constitution and showed him photos of the Soviet generals we expected would accompany Ivanovsky. I also left for him to read excerpts I had selected from Herbert Goldhamer's *The*

Soviet Soldier. The CINC and I became very comfortable with each other. This close working relationship with the general paid off on a couple of important occasions later.

By the time the Soviet party arrived in Heidelberg, I had a pretty good read on both CINCs. I felt confident that I could ask General Blanchard's staff to revise the USAREUR briefing. (Rich Kosevich and I thought the briefing should be toned down a little, as it was primarily designed for American visitors and was a little too bellicose for such a diplomatic occasion.) We recommended that such phrases as "to kill Soviet tanks" be changed in order to attain the requisite degree of diplomacy and good taste. This briefing was to be delivered in Russian, with no English translation, by Rich, who had joined me in Heidelberg during the second week of July.

My next move was to coordinate with the interpreters at the locations where the party would be visiting. Captain Joe Chachulski, then serving in a USAREUR unit, would handle Grafenwoehr. Joe had recently served at USMLM, spoke excellent Russian, and had met General Ivanovsky several times in East Germany. Major Ed Hamilton would do the briefing interpretation in Wiesbaden, and Major Bob Benning would cover the Vilseck Tank Repair Facility. They too spoke excellent Russian and were currently students at USARI. We arranged for outstanding NCOs to actually deliver the briefings in English at each stop, with the above-named officers interpreting.

By the time of the visit, all interpreters were quite familiar with the content of the briefings they would interpret for the Soviets. Majors Hamilton and Benning later served at USMLM, so it turned out all the officer interpreters involved in the CINC-CINC visit were former, current, or future members of the Mission. We also had the services of a medical doctor, Colonel Nikita Tregubov and his wife Maria—both native speakers of Russian. Maria served as the interpreter for Mrs. Blanchard and Mrs. Ivanovskaya.

Finally, just days before the Soviets were to arrive, General Blanchard sent me out to the sites to be visited and instructed me to talk with each of the unit commanders who would be involved in the visit. I was to reiterate to them General Blanchard's insistence that they be prepared for sudden changes in the program once we arrived with the Soviets. He wanted to make sure the Soviets would have no basis for suspecting anything was "canned" or falsified, as had been the case with his visit to Wünsdorf in 1973.

On the morning of July 19th, General Ivanovsky and his party drove to Eisenach and, upon crossing into West Germany, boarded CINC USAREUR's command train for the ride to Heidelberg. General Blanchard and I met them at the Heidelberg Hauptbahnhof (main rail station). After an honors ceremony in the headquarters parking lot, General Blanchard introduced his primary staff officers. General Ivanovsky took the cue and did the same with the officers accompanying him.

Among General Blanchard's senior officers was Major General Oliver Dillard, an African-American and USAREUR's Deputy Chief of Staff for Intelligence. (He had been my boss when I was assigned to Heidelberg.) General Ivanovsky paused and talked with General Dillard a bit longer than with the other U.S. generals.

He may have been thinking about meeting another African-American general at Wünsdorf in 1973. That was Major General Frederic Davison, the senior USAREUR division commander at the time. As I stated earlier, the American CINC in 1973 was General Michael Davison. Ivanovsky had been a little confused by the fact that both generals had the same last name. General Michael Davison joked with Ivanovsky that he and Fred Davison were brothers. (I had served with General Fred Davison in Vietnam; my detachment supported his 199th Light Infantry Brigade.)

After the introductions, the two CINCs and their interpreters retired to General Blanchard's office where we had a short private conference. General Ivanovsky was very curious about all the furnishings in General Blanchard's office—a stark contrast to his own barren office back in Wünsdorf—and he was particularly interested in the flags.

"I recognize the American flag, but what are these other flags for?" he asked.

"This is the U.S. Army flag with all its battle streamers," explained General Blanchard. "This, of course, is the NATO flag and this is the flag of NATO's Central Army Group (CENTAG). I wear two hats in this job: CINC USAREUR and CINC CENTAG."

"And this?" General Ivanovsky pointed to a red flag with four white stars.

"This," explained General Blanchard, "is the flag of a four-star general." He paused and then added, "This is our flag, mine and yours, general." (Later, at Grafenwoehr, Brigadier General Lynch, the training center commander, gave General Ivanovsky a four-star flag.)

Next, in the auditorium, Major Rich Kosevich presented an overview of USAREUR. From there, we went by helicopter to Wiesbaden where we viewed several exhibits and facilities of a 4th Infantry Division brigade. This included a combat training center where U.S. soldiers fired special rounds at a screen depicting advancing enemy soldiers. The screen lit up where the "bullets" struck. The soldiers on the screen were dressed in "aggressor" uniforms, so the Soviet generals felt free to cheer when a U.S. marksman hit one. From there we moved outside and showed the Soviets a tank simulator, inside of which a screen presented a battle scene and the tank gunners went through simulated firing drills.

The next stop was in an open field where several exhibits of combat equipment were displayed. This is where the first glitch in the visit occurred. General Ivanovsky was examining a chemical defense suit worn by a soldier.

"Are these boots treated to protect you against chemical contamination?" he asked the soldier who was dressed in a full chemical defense outfit.

"No, sir," came the reply.

"Then the whole outfit is worthless," said General Ivanovsky. He then turned to one of the other soldiers at the display table.

"Let me see you put on the gas mask," he said.

The soldier must have become flustered, as he was unable to get his gas mask on quickly. Another soldier stepped up and helped the first with the mask.

"Does it take two people to put on a mask?" asked Ivanovsky.

"No. This is the 'buddy method'," the second soldier cleverly responded. "It's faster this way."

General Blanchard was watching all this and I could tell he was a little upset. But he didn't interfere and we moved on to the next table. He later told me I was right about him being upset, but he decided that perhaps, in the end, it was good for the overall credibility of the exhibits and demonstrations.

Photo 30: General Ivanovsky inspects U.S. chemical defense gear.

In the mess hall General Ivanovsky walked through the chow line with the soldiers. He was fascinated by one soldier who was building a Dagwood sandwich and by another who, beside his plate of food had only a glass of water.

"Why would you drink water, when you have Coca-Cola, milk, and orange juice available in the machines?" he asked the soldier.

The soldier looked up (didn't jump up to attention) and replied, "I like water, sir."

On our way out of the mess hall, I overheard General Ivanovsky talking quietly to his chief of engineers, General Kushnikov.

"I want you to remember what you saw in there," he said. "It's not so much what they were eating, but the way everything was organized. Did you hear how they provide meals for their soldiers any hour of the day or night?"

After visiting a barracks, which General Ivanovsky said resembled more a hotel than a barracks, we flew by helicopter back to Heidelberg.

Photo 31: General Ivanovsky views a stack of M-16 rifles. The tall interpreter in the middle is Major Ed Hamilton. The Soviet officer on the far left is Senior Lieutenant Yegorov, the Soviet interpreter.

Photo 32: General Ivanovsky talks with an American soldier. The captain doing the interpreting is Joe Chachulsky.

That evening General Blanchard hosted a formal dinner. Among the gifts General Blanchard presented to his guest was a subscription to *National Geographic*. We had it addressed to General Ivanovsky, in care of the Mission. That way, we thought, it could be sent via the U.S. Army Post Office (APO) system and we could use its delivery to the Soviet general as an excuse to visit the GSFG headquarters on a monthly basis. That plan didn't work out, however, as we ended up passing it to CINC GSFG via SERB. A few months into the subscription, an envelope from a magazine company arrived at the Mission, addressed to the general. On the outside of the envelope, in bold letters, was the statement "Yes, you Evgenii Ivanovsky and four others on your street may have qualified for a one-million-dollar jackpot." We never delivered that envelope, or for that matter any of the other junk mail addressed to General Ivanovsky.

Before dinner General Blanchard engaged several of the Soviet officers in conversation. The first was General Novoseletsky, GSFG Deputy Chief of Staff.

"I hope you enjoyed this afternoon's demonstrations," said General Blanchard. "What was it you found most interesting?"

General Novoseletsky looked at General Blanchard for a moment, then looked down at the floor. "Yes. Yes, of course I enjoyed everything. But I was surprised to see such a combination of discipline and democracy in your soldiers," he replied, slowly shaking his head.

Later, General Blanchard and I moved to another group of Soviets, to whom General Novoseletsky had also attached himself. General Blanchard approached General Novoseletsky again.

"What was it you found most interesting today, General?"

I translated the question as "I'm very pleased you found the afternoon interesting." Then I gently nudged General Blanchard in the side and whispered, "We just talked to him. Choose another general." This was one case where our development of mutual trust paid off.

Another example was during General Blanchard's toast at dinner. The general had a major on his staff who, among other duties, worked as a speechwriter. He had written the toast for the CINC. I had not seen it in advance. When General Blanchard began to speak, I could see there was going to be a problem. His toast contained several inappropriate phrases, such as USAREUR "meeting the Soviet threat," "communist forces," and other undiplomatic phrases. I had to quickly decide how to interpret those remarks. I knew that if General Blanchard had had time to review his notes more thoroughly, he wouldn't have wanted to say anything that would offend his guests.

I began to make small changes in the general's remarks in my interpretation for the Soviet audience. I could see the Soviet interpreter, Lieutenant Yegorov, was confused. He probably wasn't sure if he understood the English correctly and this clearly bothered him. My own interpreters seated throughout the dining room, however, were nodding their heads. They came up to me afterwards and congratulated me on my revisions.

The next day I went to the CINC's office and talked with General Blanchard's aide-de-camp. I explained what I had done with the toast and why I thought it was necessary. The aide said that I had done the right thing. I felt somewhat guilty, however, for having changed the wording of the CINC's remarks. I thought of the interpreter in the movie "Patton," when General Patton said he didn't want to drink a toast with the Soviet general or "any other Russian son-of-a-bitch." I didn't believe General Blanchard's sentiments were the same as those of General Patton. I vowed to myself that I would try to get a preview of General Blanchard's scheduled remarks for the next dinner when we would be in Frankfurt at SMLM-F.

During the after-dinner entertainment, General Blanchard joined the 7th Army Choir for a couple of Russian songs. In one of them, I had coached the CINC to sing a solo line in Russian. Major Kosevich and I had both worked with the choir, who sang a couple of Russian songs. During the singing of the American spiritual "Amen," Mrs. Ivanovskaya joined in the rhythmic clapping. When the choir sang the "Battle Hymn of the Republic," first Mrs. Ivanovskaya and then General Ivanovsky himself joined in, as everyone sang the chorus: "Glory, glory, hallelujah." Later in the evening, I heard General Ivanovsky humming that chorus to himself.

Photo 33: General Blanchard singing a line in Russian with the 7th Army Choir.

Photo 34: General Blanchard chats with Mrs. Ivanovskaya.

As the evening wound down, General Blanchard turned to his guest. "We have a full day tomorrow, General. Is there anything in particular you would like to see?"

General Ivanovsky thought for a moment, then answered: "Yes, I'd like to see a soldier's store."

"Any kind in particular. We have a PX—a post exchange—and a commissary."

"I'd like to see a store where the soldiers go to buy their everyday things."

"I'll see to it that we do just that tomorrow," promised General Blanchard.

The next morning we flew by Army fixed-wing aircraft to Grafenwoehr, site of the 7th Army Training Center. (In the summer of 1976, in preparation for my later encounters with Soviet combat units in the field, I had spent a week here observing U.S. Army units going through their paces in field exercises.) At Grafenwoehr the Soviets were shown a wide array of combat demonstrations, including the "hip-shoot" or "hasty mission" firing by a 155mm self-propelled artillery unit that I mentioned in Chapter 21. We also watched a Cobra helicopter gunship fire a live TOW missile at tanks. Next came a series of static displays of M60A1 tanks, M113 armored personnel carriers (APC), and a TOW missile-firing simulator. General Vorobiov was given a ride in a tank; General Novoseletsky rode in the APC.

Photo 35: Soviet guests watch a live Tow-Cobra firing. The three officers to General Ivanovsky's right are: Soviet Major General Kushnikov, U.S. Colonel Tregubov, and Soviet Lieutenant General Shkidchenko. On the far right of the picture, using binoculars, is Soviet Major General Novoseletsky.

A tank had been set up for General Ivanovsky to get in and fire live rounds. He had been a tanker from the time he entered the Red Army in 1936 through 1956, when he commanded a tank division. General Shkidchenko, GSFG Chief of Combat Training, complained that he wanted to fire live rounds also. General Blanchard heard this and quickly gave one of his subordinates instructions to set up a tank for Shkidchenko. In a few moments, the loaded tank was ready for Shkidchenko, which should have demonstrated to him and the other Soviets how flexible we were about their visit. General Ivanovsky scored hits on both rounds he fired. When complimented by his entourage about his marksmanship, Ivanovsky replied, "Hell, there was nothing to it. It was all done by computer. All I had to do was push the right buttons."

A somewhat embarrassing event occurred for me at the tank maintenance school. The space was limited, so after the initial briefing, which Major Benning interpreted for the Soviets, the party split into two groups. Major Benning went with a group that began examining some of the tank repair equipment. I was left as the only U.S. interpreter with the two CINCs. General Ivanovsky wanted to look over an M60A1 tank. I wasn't prepared to handle the technical terminology the sergeant began to use in explaining various aspects of the equipment. I turned to Lieutenant Yegorov and said, "You take over." Lieutenant Yegorov was equally caught by surprise. As he worked at interpreting the sergeant's remarks, General Ivanovsky corrected him from time to time. After awhile, I took pity on Yegorov and took over the job. I too faltered now and then, at which times General Ivanovsky would smile and give me the Russian word for a part of the tank he knew very well from his own tanker days.

A couple of particularly interesting things occurred at Grafenwoehr that had nothing to do with military equipment. During noon meal in a field tent, one of the Soviet generals sitting apart from the two CINCs, began questioning U.S. officers about drug abuse in USAREUR. When we left the mess tent, General Ivanovsky overheard the conversation that had continued as the generals were walking out after the meal. He whirled around and addressed his generals.

"Who brought up that topic?" he demanded.

The Soviet generals went silent.

"I want to know how this conversation got started," reiterated Ivanovsky.

One of the generals stepped forward and was about to confess, when General Blanchard interrupted.

"No, General Ivanovsky, that's all right. I want you to be able to broach any subject. Drug abuse is an important matter."

General Blanchard then gave the Soviets a short rundown of USAREUR's progress in combating the use of drugs by its soldiers. He asked a couple of his own commanders to explain what they were doing in their own units. None of the Soviet generals asked any questions. General Blanchard turned to General Ivanovsky.

"Do you have any questions about this issue, General?"

"No, no, no," replied Ivanovsky. "You've given us a very complete and frank explanation. I think we know all we need to about your drug abuse programs."

Photo 36: The author leaving the field mess at Grafenwoehr with General Ivanovsky.

It is interesting to speculate whether General Ivanovsky recalled this discussion several years later when Soviet soldiers in Afghanistan got involved in drugs. Many of them became addicted. Soldiers who returned to the Soviet Union brought narcotics and habits with them that contributed to the start of the currently serious drug problem in the Russian Army and Russian society as a whole.

Photo 37: General Blanchard encourages an open discussion about the drug problems and solutions in USAREUR. To my immediate right is Soviet Senior Lieutenant Yegorov; behind me, the tall officer is Major General Vorobiov.

Later, as we were walking toward the Post Exchange, General Ivanovsky spotted a Stars and Stripes store—a store that specialized in newspapers, magazines and books for soldiers and their families.

"Can we go into that store?" asked General Ivanovsky.

"Of course," said General Blanchard.

The party turned and headed for the store. Inside, the manager met us. While he was talking to General Ivanovsky, the other Soviet generals quickly found the adult reading section. They scarfed up copies of *Playboy* and *Penthouse*, opened them and stood looking at the "articles." I was with the CINCs, so I didn't hear what the other generals said about what they were viewing, but one of the other interpreters later told me General Vorobiov said, "I'm too old for this." (Still, if you remember, he was too young to be my grandfather!)

As we were preparing to leave Grafenwoehr, General Ivanovsky asked if he could see an NCO apartment. General Blanchard smiled and said he would see what he could do. He discovered that one of our drivers lived at Graf, so General Blanchard asked him if his wife was German. When the sergeant said "no," the CINC requested that we be permitted to see his quarters. The sergeant readily agreed and immediately called his wife. You can imagine what might have been going through her head when her husband explained that CINC USAREUR and a bunch of Russian generals were coming to visit!

General Blanchard knew that Mrs. Ivanovskaya's visit to an NCO quarters the day before in Heidelberg had not turned out too well. The NCO's wife was German, which Mrs. Ivanovskaya apparently resented, saying "This is not an American apartment, it's German." Her attitude toward Germans tracked with my experiences in East Germany where Soviet disdain for Germans often made itself known, both on an official and unofficial basis.

There were only four passengers in our plane that flew from Grafenwoehr to Frankfurt. The two CINCs sat side by side across an aisle and the two interpreters sat facing them. General Ivanovsky was very quiet and spent most of the flight simply looking out the window at the German landscape below. When I noticed General Blanchard take some 3 x 5 cards from his pocket and begin to read them, I asked him what they were. He told me they were notes for his toast that night at the SMLM-F reception and dinner. I asked if I could see them. He handed them to me. I took out a pencil and made a few, slight changes. Then I handed them back to him and waited for his reaction. He looked at the cards for a few minutes.

"So you really think I should use your changes?"

"Yes, sir."

"Fine. They look good to me."

That night I was able to interpret the CINC's remarks without any editorial revisions.

The highlight of the evening at SMLM-F occurred when, during a conversation between the CINCs, General Ivanovsky sent Lieutenant Yegorov away by telling him, "Go get something to eat." With Yegorov gone, there remained only the two CINCs and I as their interpreter.

"General Blanchard," Ivanovsky began, "I want you to know how much I appreciate what you've done for me and my staff. I looked carefully for signs that events were being staged, but all I saw were realistic demonstrations and open access to your officers and soldiers. You obviously have a well-trained army in which you have a lot of confidence. This visit has been one of the highlights of my career."

General Blanchard accepted those remarks as proof to himself that his plan had worked. No matter the politics of the day or the near future, Ivanovsky was one important Soviet general who would go home with a new appreciation for the U.S. Army in Europe.

To the best of my knowledge, the Soviets had never before been treated so warmly, nor had they been given such free access to the soldiers and actual military hardware of the U.S. Army. In all likelihood, due to their lifelong indoctrination of anti-American propaganda, CINC USAREUR's candor and flexibility must have stunned or perplexed the entire Soviet party. No army would be so open and allow such freedom of movement to a possible enemy, if it were not sure of itself. CINC GSFG frequently said such things as "very clever," "very practical," "very impressive."

General Ivanovsky's opinion of USAREUR certainly didn't correspond to the press or intelligence reports he was accustomed to reading about a demoralized, undisciplined and unpatriotic army. I can't say with any certainty what the practical results of General Ivanovsky's impressions were, but his later promotion to CINC Soviet Ground Forces may have led to the application within the Soviet Army of several principles he observed during his visit to USAREUR.

CHAPTER 23
LOOKING BACK

In early September, 1977, I received orders to report to the Pentagon. I was being assigned to a special study group. The group—Review of Education and Training for Officers (RETO)—was to make recommendations on future officer training to the Army Chief of Staff, General Bernard Rogers. My initial reaction was disappointment that I would be unable to finish my two years at the Mission. When informed, however, that the leader of this small study group, Major General Ben Harrison, had handpicked me because of my education, knowledge of foreign languages, and experience with the Soviet military, I realized this new assignment was an honor. General Harrison had used Army Chief of Staff authority to curtail for RETO the assignments of some battalion and brigade commanders as well. I would be responsible for making recommendations regarding U.S. Army officer education in foreign languages, would research and report on foreign military officer schooling, and address the question of specialists vs. generalists in the future U.S. Army. It sounded like a great challenge. Still, if I had been given a choice in the matter, I would have asked to stay at USMLM.

In the relatively short time I had served at the Mission, I had learned a great deal about the Soviet Army and military intelligence collection. But I had not yet made a dent in what I believed I could accomplish, especially with the SANDDUNE project beginning to take on added importance. When I thought about the intelligence aspects of my touring in East Germany—what I had actually produced—I had serious doubts that I had contributed anything really important.

I had several questions about whether any of USMLM's collection efforts warranted the dangers we often faced during our tours throughout East Germany. So a Mission tour ran a column of 200 vehicles and wrote down the vehicles' VRNs. So a Mission team got photographs of an installation that either showed or didn't show new military equipment. What did that mean for the larger intelligence picture? When the T-64 tank was introduced into GSFG, were we the only ones who could find out its technical characteristics with our photography? If we learned that the ethnic makeup of GSFG was primarily Slavic or Central Asian, did that help our intelligence analysts better assess the capabilities of the Soviet Army in East Germany?

At the time, I didn't attempt to answer these questions for myself, as I had to report to the Pentagon in less than ten days. My immediate tasks were to clear my desk of intelligence reports (IIRs) and to make arrangements for my family to move to Washington, DC. I didn't have time to review my IIRs at USMLM—to take stock of the quantity or quality of my reporting—or even to think much about what I had witnessed over the last 14 months.

Over the next few years, however, I often thought about whether my service and USMLM operations in general had been worthwhile. Looking back today, I can say without any reservations that I believe USMLM made a major contribution to the prevention of a ground war involving NATO forces. There were, of course, many other factors that figured into the war vs. peace equation, especially at the strategic level. But the Soviet Army and Air Force in East Germany would have had a crucial role in any Soviet attack on NATO. The Mission's presence and activities had to have been a factor in deterring Soviet recklessness. In the event of war, the intelligence gained from USMLM reporting would have helped us more effectively counter the Soviet Army. Just to have been a member of such an organization went a long way toward satisfying my need to know I had participated in a valuable operation.

By the end of my service at USMLM, I had become convinced that intelligence (military intelligence in particular) was the front line of defense for the United States. The Communist Party of the Soviet Union had consolidated its power after the 1917 October "Revolution," (and maintained it) only by the use of military or police force. The USSR had expanded its empire into Eastern Europe, and continued to maintain it, once again, only by the use of military and police force. (In fact, it was military force that made it possible for the Russian empire even before the Bolshevik "Revolution" to gain and maintain its dominance on the Eurasian land mass.)

There was no doubt in my mind that the military component of Russian and Soviet power was vital. Therefore, military intelligence directed against the Soviets took on more significance than against any other country. My assignment at USMLM gave me the opportunity to personally wage battle with the Soviet military in the intelligence war that never ends. After years of "book learning," the Mission had given me the opportunity to learn firsthand something about the nuts and bolts of the Soviet Army and its officers and men.

Being alert to IOH was the first priority among USMLM's classified intelligence tasks (See Chapter 12). But military intelligence is a multifaceted discipline. In addition to IOH, military intelligence has two primary tasks: 1) to reveal the military strengths and weaknesses of a potential enemy in order to help prepare our own forces for combat, should that need arise, and 2) to lay the groundwork for our own policymakers and military leaders, as well as those of the potential enemy, to correctly assess each other's strengths and weaknesses. USMLM contributed to both these missions.

In carrying out the first task, USMLM covered fixed and mobile targets that provided personnel and equipment details, as well as identification of Soviet and East German units and military installations. In other words, USMLM provided theater and national level leaders order of battle information: Who and where are the enemy's units? What are his personnel and technical capabilities? The Mission provided up-to-date information on the training it observed and, especially, on the military technology GSFG was using in the field. The nitty-gritty facts both Ground and Air Teams at the Mission were able to discover through close-up observation and photography told our military leaders in Europe and Washington what they would have to do to counter Soviet combat technology. Some intelligence collection missions may have seemed trivial at times to me, to a few other tour officers, or outside observers. But now I can see that the accumulation over several years of technical information about the GSFG units and their combat equipment filled in many critical pieces in the puzzle for analysts and policymakers at higher headquarters.

The second task of military intelligence is not always so obvious. I'm convinced that good intelligence collection and analysis can also help to avoid miscalculations that might cause counterproductive policies or mistakenly lead to war. USMLM played a crucial role in avoiding miscalculation by either the U.S. or the Soviets. This is extremely important but I believe it is not fully appreciated.

Miscalculations are often preventable mistakes. They arise from one's preconceptions or ignorance of the facts, thus leading one side to wrongly anticipate what the other side might do in a particular situation. Often this derives from mirror-imaging—the tendency for one to assume others think like *we* do, that they will use what *we* consider "common sense" and, consequently, will not do anything *we* think is stupid. Mirror-imaging is a natural recourse when analysts do not understand the language and culture of the opposing side. That is one reason why the FAO program was so important to the Mission's success and continues to be an important element of our analysis at the various levels of the Army.

At the national level, ignorance of the other side's likely reactions can have disastrous consequences. Murphy argues that Soviet miscalculation of Allied resolve during the 1948-49 Berlin blockade, combined with their misjudgment of the effect of the Korean War on the United States and Europe "laid the foundation for the strategic confrontation that dominated the Cold War until its end." I might add that U.S. inaction, as events unfolded in Afghanistan in the late 1970s, was based on our own ignorance of the Soviets' perceived need to have a reliable ally on their southern border. A miscalculation of defense needs, as perceived by the Soviets, led to our surprise when the Soviets invaded Afghanistan in 1979.

USMLM collection and reporting from 1947 onward did much to diminish any ignorance or prejudice that might lead to miscalculation in U.S. intelligence circles. The Mission was able to dispel the myth that the Soviet soldier was "ten feet tall" and invincible. At the same time, USMLM reports clearly showed the Soviet soldier and, especially his officers, were not just crude peasants who relied on brute strength rather than sophisticated equipment and tactics to fight a war. I dare say no veteran of USMLM came away from that assignment without a genuine respect for the Soviet fighting machine.

Operation Cervine Twist, the visit to West Germany by General Ivanovsky, went a long way toward clearing up many misconceptions the Soviet general and his staff may have had about the American soldier and the U.S. Army in Europe. I'm convinced the impressions and conclusions Ivanovsky took back to his headquarters, and later to the Moscow Defense Staff, played an important part in preventing the Soviets from underestimating

USAREUR. Much of the credit for this goes to General George Blanchard himself; however, Mission officers in Berlin and West Germany during the visit provided important assistance in planning and carrying out that operation successfully. I believe there should have been many more military-to-military exchanges and not only between CINCs. In one of his toasts during Cervine Twist, General Blanchard said, "Only by talking can we begin to find ways to understand each other better. Not to talk is to risk misunderstandings that could prove tragic for everyone."

The very presence of fourteen U.S. military personnel (as well as those of the other Allied Missions) who toured, observed and photographed Soviet military activities and facilities was a significant step toward preventing Soviet miscalculation. The Soviets knew what the Mission was doing and had to conclude we knew much about their organization, equipment, and operations. Given the tendency of intelligence analysts to "worst-case" their findings, the Soviets may even have overestimated how much we knew about them.

Allen Dulles wrote in his *Craft of Intelligence* that "the fact that intelligence is alert, that there is a possibility of forewarning, could itself constitute one of the most effective deterrents to a potential enemy's appetite for attack." John Piña Craven, in his *The Silent War*, adds that "The intelligence game is fearful and wonderful. Both sides will never believe anything that they have not confirmed through intelligence. Therefore, if you wish to give a message... you have to allow access to the adversary so that he can see for himself that the [information] is credible."

Thus, USMLM's and the other Allied Missions' value as overt, publicly identifiable, intelligence collection organizations that must have seemed to the Soviets at times to be "everywhere," surely factored into Soviet intentions and planning. It was a case of "they knew we knew" who they were, where they were, and what their strengths and weaknesses were. Craven's conclusion is supported by a statement of one BRIXMIS officer who, in discussing the Berlin Wall crisis, remarked "Everything we saw we were meant to see, so the message was unequivocal! That's just what the Allied Military Missions were for. Maybe... we have in our own minuscule way played a part in preventing the Third World War."

Although it's clear to all us former 'missionaries' that we saw a few things we weren't supposed to see, it's also true that during the perestroika years, well after my departure from USMLM, Soviet leader Gorbachev appears to have used this strategy. In order to convince the West that the military aspects of his reforms were genuine, the Soviets reopened PRAs in 1988 that had been closed in 1984. Thus, Allied Military Liaison Missions were able to better observe what was going on within GSFG.

On a personal note, my experiences at USMLM provided some lasting lessons and challenges for the future. The most interesting and significant development for me was that I had become more devoted to intelligence than to foreign languages. My Russian at USMLM had become only a tool for my work in intelligence. Although that was true also of my duty with ASA at Teufelsberg, during my time at USMLM, for the first time in my Army career, I thought little about my language studies. I took no Russian courses, as I was spending all my available "study" time learning the technical aspects of the Soviet military and its equipment. By now, intelligence had become for me almost a form of religion. There seemed to me to be no other comparable calling that carried such urgency and purpose. I came to believe that intelligence was one of the most noble professions. I still believe that today.

In addition to the religious-like moral or philosophical perspective I had taken toward intelligence, another factor also attracted me. Especially now that I had served at USMLM. That was the excitement and gratification of being involved in an endeavor that was real, important, and ongoing every day. I am reminded of a fellow officer with whom I served at West Point. Mike was an infantry captain who had served three tours in Vietnam with the 101st Airborne and U.S. Special Forces. He had a Distinguished Service Cross, several Silver Stars and Purple Hearts. One day he stopped me in the hallway and asked me what I thought about his transferring to Military Intelligence.

"Why would you want to do that, Mike?"

"Well," he said, "The war's over in Vietnam. I'm afraid my career from now on is going to be boring."

"What do you mean?"

"I'll probably do nothing more interesting in the coming years than jump out of an airplane a few times and 'practice' war on training exercises."

"And you think MI will be more interesting?"

"Yes, you MI guys are always closer to the powder keg. You always have something going on, whether it's peacetime or wartime."

Although perhaps not as exciting as Mike thought for everyone in Military Intelligence, he had a point. A point that attracted me also. Intelligence was a "24-7" occupation, to use today's vernacular. There was, indeed, always something to do that we were confident was important. We believed we were on the front line of the Cold War. At the Mission, we were even behind the potential front line.

As an intelligence officer, my time at the Mission made me realize I was more inclined toward analysis than collection. I was grateful for the opportunity to be a collector, but I believed I was more productive as an analyst. Years later, I found a passage in Allen Dulles' *The Craft of Intelligence* that could have been a variation of a horoscope for me. Dulles wrote that "A man who is more interested in intellectual pursuits than in people, in observation and thought than in action, will make a better 'analyst' than an 'operator.' For this reason, it is no surprise that people from the academic professions fill many of the analytic jobs..." The analytic background I brought to my tasks as a tour officer was greatly overshadowed by the value of those intelligence collection experiences I would be bringing back with me to future analytic jobs. My professional "schooling" as a Soviet political-military specialist had continued in a realistic, concrete, "hands-on" environment.

I had seen Soviet units and combat equipment in training, as well as in many of their daily routines. I had met face-to-face with Soviet officers and soldiers. I was not entirely shocked, but was disappointed to learn that Soviet officers—those "political activists," most of whom were members of the Communist Party—accepted what they read in *Krasnaya zvezda*, the central newspaper of the Russian military. I knew how writers in that newspaper characterized American society and the U.S. Armed Forces. It was unabashedly negative and misinformed, sometimes inflammatory, especially during the Vietnam War era.

In my conversations with most Soviet officers, it was clear that to them being a good Communist was the same thing as being a Soviet patriot. They saw no conflicts in their allegiances and their worldviews. Their daily indoctrination since childhood, and especially the intensive political classes they continued to attend in their military units, had purged their minds of almost all sense of criticism or doubt about what the Communist Party taught. As I looked forward to analytic positions in the future, I concluded there was not, and probably would never be, such a thing as an Army-Party rift.

On the other hand, many of the Soviet officers I met were otherwise professional, cultured and gracious to USMLM members. One could sense in them a hint of suppressed admiration or envy for our status as Americans in a free and, especially, economically thriving nation. One officer in particular—Lieutenant Colonel Igor Kanavin, Chief of SERB during my last months at USMLM—always presented himself in an unassuming, pleasant manner. His wife stood out from the other Soviet wives with her Western clothing. Both Colonel and Mrs. Kanavin gave me the impression they were very comfortable in the company of U.S. officers at social functions. Colonel Kanavin would also discreetly help me out when I needed a word in Russian during my interpreting duties at social functions. I would meet him a few years later under entirely different circumstances.

Although by now I viewed my Russian as simply a tool for intelligence work, my Russian language skills nevertheless had provided me with the opportunity to play an important role in many aspects of the Mission's work. Russian was the starting point for my intelligence career. It was Russian that put me at the listening position on Teufelsberg for the RB-66 shoot-down in 1964. It was Russian that made me a better collector and analyst of SANDDUNE materials. It was Russian that put me in the middle of Cervine Twist. My experience with Cervine Twist turned out not only to be a major highlight of my assignment at USMLM (and of my career), it may have been the event in which I made the most substantive contribution while at the Mission. My association with General Ivanovsky and the generals on his staff put a human face to the marshals, generals, and admirals I had studied about (and would continue to study) in high-level Kremlin political and military intrigues.

Russian had turned me into an intelligence sergeant and later an intelligence officer. It was almost by accident, since other than teaching, intelligence was the most productive field in which the Army could use my language skills. But although I had Russian to thank for getting me into intelligence, the language now became secondary. By the time I left USMLM, I was an intelligence officer first, a Russian linguist second.

For those of us who served at USMLM during the Cold War years, there may be no other assignment that gave us the sense of accomplishment we enjoyed in Potsdam and Berlin. Some fifteen years later, when the

Soviet Union imploded and there was a flurry of business and intergovernmental activity in the new Russia, both Army and Air Force veterans of USMLM made up an already trained contingent of qualified personnel from which American companies and the U.S. government were able to choose cadre to represent them in Moscow.

The true value of the Mission's work that resulted from the dedication and sacrifice of a few hundred men and women may never be fully known. There is evidence enough, however, that USMLM was a key player in the East-West confrontation in Europe during the Cold War. My personal contributions to intelligence assessments of Soviet order of battle, the acquisition of technical data or the prevention of miscalculation on either side may have been modest. But it is enough for me to know I helped in some small way.

Appendix A
Huebner-Malinin Agreement

AGREEMENT

ON MILITARY LIAISON MISSIONS ACCREDITED TO THE SOVIET AND UNITED STATES COMMANDERS IN CHIEF OF THE ZONES OF OCCUPATION IN GERMANY

In conformity with the provisions of Article 2 of the Agreement on "Control Mechanism in Germany", dated November 14, 1944, the United States and the Soviet Commanders in Chief of the zones of Occupation in Germany have agreed to exchange Military Liaison Missions accredited to their staffs in the zones and approve the following regulations concerning these missions:

1. These missions are military missions and have no authority over quadripartite military government missions or purely military government missions of each respective country, either temporarily or permanently, on duty in either zone. However, they will render whatever

aid or assistance to said military government missions as is practicable.

2.   Missions will be composed of air, navy and army representatives. There will be no political representative.

3.   The missions will consist of not to exceed fourteen (14) officers and enlisted personnel. This number will include all necessary technical personnel, office clerks, personnel with special qualifications, and personnel required to operate radio stations.

4.   Each mission will be under the order of the senior member of the mission who will be appointed and known as "Chief of the United States (or Soviet) Military Mission".

5.   The Chief of the mission will be accredited to the Commander in Chief of the occupation forces.

In the United States zone the mission will be accredited to Commander in Chief, United States European Command.

In the Soviet zone the mission will be accredited to the Commander in Chief of the Group of Soviet Occupational Forces in Germany.

6.   In the United States zone the Soviet Mission will be offered quarters in the region of Frankfurt.

7.   In the Soviet zone the United States Mission will be offered quarters at or near Potsdam.

8. In the United States zone the Chief of the Soviet Mission will communicate with A/C of Staff, G-3, United States European Command.

9. In the Soviet zone the Chief of the United States Mission will communicate with the Senior Officer of the Staff of Commander in Chief.

10. Each member of the missions will be given identical travel facilities to include identical permanent passes in Russian and English languages permitting complete freedom of travel wherever and whenever it will be desired over territory and roads in both zones, except places of disposition of military units, without escort or supervision.

Each time any member of Soviet or United States mission wants to visit United States or Soviet headquarters, military government offices, forces, units, military schools, factories and enterprises which are under United States or Soviet control, a corresponding request must be made to Director, Operations, Plans, Organization and Training, European Command, or Senior Officer, Headquarters, Group of Soviet Occupational Forces in Germany. Such requests must be acted upon within 24-72 hours.

Members of the missions are permitted allied guests at the headquarters of the respective missions.

11. a. Each mission will have its own radio station for communication with its own headquarters.

b. In each case couriers and messengers will be given facilities for free travel between the headquarters of the mission and headquarters of their respective Commanders-in-Chief. These couriers will enjoy the same immunity which is extended to diplomatic couriers.

c. Each mission will be given facilities for telephone communication through the local telephone exchange at the headquarters, and they also will be given facilities such as mail, telephone, telegraph through the existing means of communication when the members of the mission will be traveling within the zone. In case of a breakdown in the radio installation, the zone commanders will render all possible aid and will permit temporary use of their own systems of communications.

12. The necessary rations, P.O.L. supplies and household services for the military missions will be provided for by the headquarters to which accredited, by method of mutual compensation in kind, supplemented by such items as desired to be furnished by their own headquarters.

In addition the respective missions or individual members of the missions may purchase items of Soviet or United States origin which must be paid for in currency specified by the headquarters controlling zone where purchase is made.

13. The buildings of each mission will enjoy full right of extra-territoriality.

14. a. The task of the mission will be to maintain liaison between both Commanders in Chief and their staffs.

b. In each zone the mission will have the right to engage in matters of protecting the interests of their nationals and to make representations accordingly, as well as in matters of protecting their property interests in the zone where they are located. They have the right to render aid to people of their own country who are visiting the zone where they are accredited.

15. This agreement may be changed or amplified by mutual consent to cover new subjects when the need arises.

16. This agreement is written in russian and english languages and both texts are authentic.

17. This agreement becomes valid when signed by Deputy Commanders of United States and Soviet Zones of Occupation.

Lieutenant General HUEBNER	Colonel General MALININ
Deputy Commander in Chief European Command.	Deputy Commander in Chief Chief of Staff of the Group of Soviet Occupation Forces in Germany
	/dated/ 5 April 1947

Author's note: The style and inconsistencies in punctuation and capitalization suggest the English version was translated from the Russian.

Appendix B
Glossary of Foreign Terms Used in this Book

Russian

Akt	[Here] An official document outlining the situation and the reason for a detention.
Bol'shoe spasibo	Many thanks.
Da	Yes.
Demob	Short for demobilizatsiya, 'demobilization'.
Dlya sluzhebnogo potrebleniya	For Official Use Only.
Dyedushka	Grandpa.
Dyevushka	Girl.
I vy govorite po-russki khorosho?	And you speak Russian well?
Khorosho	Good, fine.
Komendant	Similar to U.S. provost marshal, Soviet military police in charge of city area. USMLM unit histories use the spelling 'kommandant'.

Komendatura	Office of the komendant. USMLM histories use the spelling 'kommandatura.'
Mat	Russian slang for serious profanity.
Nichevo	Nothing. Don't mention it.
Podpolkovnik	Lieutenant colonel.
Praporschik	Soviet warrant officer.
PZR	Soviet abbreviation for a Permanent Restricted Area (postoyannij zapretnyj rajon).
Razumeesh' po-russki?	Do you understand Russian?
Razumeyu	I understand.
Shpion	Spy.
Spasibo	Thank you.
Stoika	Stance, Standing position.
Strelyayut	[You] will be shot (in this context).
Tovarisch	Comrade.
Tovarisch po...	...mate.
UAZ	Soviet jeep-like vehicle (there were two: UAZ-69 and UAZ-469).
VZR	Soviet abbreviation for Temporary Restricted Area (Vremennyj zapretnyj rajon).
Yaitsa	Eggs, Russian slang for testicles.
Yest'	"Yes, sir" in answer to a command.
Zdes'	Here.

French

Beaucoup
'Much' or 'many'. Learned from the Vietnamese during our war there. French was spoken widely among the upper classes in Vietnam before the Indochina wars. Vietnam veterans and their friends and families still use the term occasionally.

Raison d'être
Reason for existing, being.

German

Ach, mein Gott!
Oh, my God!

Danke
Thanks.

Ein Bier, bitte
A beer, please.

Gaststätte
German pub

Hauptbahnhof
Main rail station.

Hier
Here.

  Wird geschossen
[You] will be shot.

Ich bin ein
I'm a

  Berliner
Berliner. (President Kennedy's German translator gave him the phrase incorrectly. What he should have said was "Ich bin Berliner." The way it came out, the president said, "I'm a jelly donut.")

Ja
Yes.

Kiste
Box (for tour personnel, a box full of food and drink).

Parkplatz
Wayside or rest area along German highways.

Sind Sie Amerikaner?	Are you Americans?
Sprechen Sie Deutsch?	Do you speak German?
Wehrmacht	World War II German Armed Forces.
Kaserne	Barracks.

Appendix C

KGB-Approved Memo Instructing Soviet Military Duty Officers What to Do Upon Sighting an Allied Military Liaison Mission Vehicle
(Source: USMLM Association Website. Translation by author)

Approved
Senior operative of the Special Section,
KGB, USSR

Borovikov

INSTRUCTIONS

to the unit duty officer on procedures to be used when detaining foreign military mission personnel

The duty officer and his assistant, upon receiving word from komendant-service personnel, the police or servicemen that a foreign military liaison mission car is approaching the garrison's military installations, must find out from them the time, location, direction of movement and the identity of the missionaries, after which he must immediately inform the unit's chief of staff and his assistant, as well as the KGB operative.

Members of foreign missions are REQUIRED:

to respect the laws of the GDR, maintain the public order and strictly observe the traffic regulations of public transport established in the GDR;

unconditionally carry out the orders of military auto-inspection representatives, barriers and traffic controls set up by troop units of the WGF and NVA of the GDR, including GDR police;

while located in the GDR to always be in the uniform of their army with their appropriate rank insignia;

to travel only in vehicles of their own missions, displaying on the front and back special license plates with writing in Russian/American, French, British/ military missions and showing a picture of the flags of their respective country;

the license plates on foreign liaison mission vehicles are allotted as follows:

Nos. 1 - 12 — British MLM
Nos. 20 - 29 — American MLM
Nos. 30 - 39 — French MLM

Members of foreign liaison missions are FORBIDDEN:
entry into permanent or temporary restricted areas, as well as the territory of troop units, training areas, firing

ranges, airfields and other military installations of WGF, NVA and industrial facilities of the GDR;

observation of military posts, airfields, training areas and other military installations of WGF, NVA, as well as railway stations during both the loading and unloading of troops and military equipment;

following troop columns of WGF, NVA of the GDR, as well as observation of them off main roads and highways, travel at dark in vehicles with foreign or unlighted license plates;

photography of troops and combat equipment of WGF and NVA of the GDR, military and industrial installations, drawing pictures or diagrams, taking notes or making recordings of an intelligence nature;

the use of equipment for intelligence purposes;
the transport in mission vehicles of personnel not belonging to the missions;

wearing civilian clothes in the GDR;

conducting propaganda against the USSR, GDR and other socialist countries; distribution of newspapers, brochures, leaflets and other printed material of an anti-communist nature.

CHIEF OF STAFF, UNIT POSTAL NUMBER 58696
MAJOR   ARZHILOVSKIJ

Appendix D

**Instructions to GSFG Soldiers on What to Do Upon Sighting
Allied Military Liaison Mission Vehicles**
(Source: USMLM Association Website. Translation by Author)

GSFG SOLDIER, BE VIGILANT!

INSTRUCTIONS
for actions upon observing and
detaining vehicles with members
of FMLM

Examples of license plates for FMLM vehicles

**Vehicles of the British Military Liaison Mission have
license numbers 1-15**

**Vehicles of the American Military Liaison Mission have
license numbers from 20-29**

**Vehicles of the French Military Liaison Mission have
license numbers from 30-39**

1. LEGAL STATUS OF FOREIGN MILITARY LIAISON MISSIONS ATTACHED TO CINC, GSFG

1.   The American, British and French military liaison missions are accredited and attached to the Commander in Chief of the Group of Soviet Forces, Germany.

2.   Members of the foreign military liaison missions (FMLM) are allowed free travel throughout the GDR with the exception of permanent and temporary restricted areas, locations of troop units and military installations.

Members of the FMLM are permitted to use the Autobahns that transverse restricted areas and roads that border these areas.

The boundaries of permanent and temporary restricted areas are established by CINC, GSFG.

3.   Members of the missions are allowed to travel in the GDR only in vehicles of their missions that display on the front and rear bumpers special license plates. In doing so, mission members must be in the uniform of their army and be wearing their military rank.

4.   Throughout the GDR, FMLM members do not have the right to conduct observation (with notes, recording, drawing, diagrams, or with the use of binoculars, etc). They may not observer troop movements, military installations and military equipment. Furthermore, they may not photograph or make moving pictures of the above.

II. OPERATING PROCEDURES UPON DISCOVERY OF FMLM VEHICLES AND PERSONNEL

1. Having discovered a FMLM vehicle, every serviceman must immediately report via his commander (chief) to the unit duty officer. He in turn must report this to the nearest Soviet military komendatura.

The report includes:

— which mission and the vehicle license number, the time and place of discovery (with a reference to the terrain);

— the number in the team and their uniform;

— the nature of their activities;

— the vehicle's direction of travel.

III. OPERATING PROCEDURES WHEN DETAINING VEHICLES AND MEMBERS OF FMLM

1. GSFG soldiers are required to detain the FMLM vehicle and personnel in the following situations:

— in restricted areas, locations of troop units and military installations regardless of the activities of the crews of the FMLM vehicles;

— throughout the GDR if the mission vehicle has joined columns of military equipment, if it is organizing observations (with notes and recordings) of troops and military installations, as well as photographing them.

2. The detention of FMLM vehicles and personnel should be accomplished at the place of their violation

of established rules by means of blocking their vehicle in such a way that it cannot leave the place of detention before the arrival of representatives of the Soviet military komendatura.

3. Having detained the vehicle and personnel of FMLM, soldiers are required to report to the nearest Soviet military komendatura the following information: the number of the FMLM vehicle; the makeup of the crew; the time, place and reason for the detention.

Soldiers detaining the FMLM vehicle are permitted to check the documents of the crew in order to establish their identities.

Only the military komendants have the right to determine the circumstances of the detention.

4. It is categorically forbidden to use force, weapons, or actions that might threaten the security of members of the missions. It is forbidden also to search the crew or their vehicle, to enter into conversations with mission members or explain to them the reason for their detention.

Soldiers who have detained the vehicle and members of FMLM may leave the spot of detention only with the permission of the military komendant.

Note: The provisions of this instruction pamphlet are to be disseminated for use by personnel at guard posts, specified by the UG and KS [Manual of Garrison Duties] of the Soviet Armed Forces.

KNOW AND FOLLOW STRICTLY!

Order No. 142

APPENDIX E

The Ideal Tour Officer and Tour NCO
(Based on text in 1967 USMLM Unit History)

The Tour Officer

The terms "liaison officer," "tour officer," and "recon officer" are synonymous when used to refer to the officers assigned to USMLM who are accredited to CINC GSFG and regularly travel in the Soviet Zone. Liaison Officer is a handy term, since it does not imply the intelligence information-gathering mission, while Recon Officer can be used with impunity among those who are privy to the aspects of the USMLM operation. "Tour Officer," a sort of compromise, is most commonly used, and is an outgrowth of the reference to trips into the Soviet Zone as "tours."

The tour officer must learn the geography of East Germany, especially its transportation nets and the disposition of the 26 Soviet and East German divisions located there. He must learn to identify the tremendous variety of Soviet and East German military equipment and vehicles. He must learn as much as possible about the history of USMLM operations in the Soviet Zone, and from the experience of others begin to develop a feel for the methods and techniques which have proved successful in accomplishing the missions of USMLM.

He must develop his own distillate of the ingredients of diplomacy and aggressiveness, caution and daring, circumspection and boldness, which characterize the successful, productive tour officer. He must develop to the highest possible degree his ability to react to constantly new and changing situations with actions that take into account all the complex considerations required of USMLM representatives, when the reaction must be instantaneous and time for reflection comes only afterwards. He must quickly learn the full meaning of the responsibility given him by virtue of the fact that he is representing the U.S. in East Germany. Most of the time he is alone with only his car and his driver. He knows that tour officer judgment is expected to provide good results with no incidents reflecting negatively on himself, USMLM, or his country.

He must continue to grow and develop, for there is no such thing as becoming so proficient or accomplished that the tour officer can relax and coast. The best tour officer we ever knew departed on his final trip into the Soviet Zone complaining that he felt he could have made good use of a few more hours of preparation, and returned from it with the comment, "Well, it was a pretty good trip, but I wish I were going to have a chance to go back and try to do better on this or that target." That is a Tour Officer.

The Tour NCO

The tour NCO must perform a thorough pre-departure vehicle check, assure adequate provisions, take vehicle counts when running columns, act as sentinel at operations, detect tail vehicles and accomplish other fundamental operations. There are, however, certain intangibles not specifically called for, but necessary, if the driver is to effectively make his contribution to the tour team effort.

First and foremost he must be alert. Driving skills, linguistic prowess, identification familiarization and an intimate knowledge of East Germany are no substitute for a keen and sensitive awareness. Tour driving is an ordeal; much of the time is spent patiently traversing East German roads and terrain. Boredom and fatigue set in. But the arrival of the unexpected must always be anticipated. A quick reaction can prevent an accident or retention. Quick response can result in the procurement of important intelligence data.

A tour NCO must be observant, incessantly scanning the horizon in search of pertinent discoveries. He is an invaluable aid to the tour officer, who must navigate, observe and photograph. The driver allows the Tour Officer to devote more attention to the fine points of his mission. Aside from the feeling of accomplishment, there is also the element of danger and adventure.

APPENDIX F
STASI DOSSIER EXCERPTS

In 2004, I sent a letter to the German government, requesting access to my East German *Stasi* dossier for the period 1976-77—the years I served at USMLM. I had hoped to include whatever information I received in my first edition of *Potsdam Mission*. After follow-up letters to Berlin in 2005 and 2007, I finally received some materials from the MfS central files. To my disappointment, however, there was nothing in the materials that had any bearing on my activities at USMLM. There did appear, however, some sketchy biographic information on me and my family. Here I discovered some curious and interesting data.

The curious included, together with some correct information, the following physical descriptions:

Brillenträger (starke Gläser)	Wears glasses with heavy lenses
sommersprossiges Gesicht	freckled face
Asiatische Züge	Asiatic appearance
leichte Hakennase	slightly crooked nose
hinkt rechts	limps with right leg

Three pages from a partial *Stasi* dossier sent to me by the German government.

If a *Stasi* agent were to rely only on these characteristics to pick me up for surveillance, I could have walked right by him without being noticed.

There were two particular entries that I found interesting. The first was that my address was listed for when I served at the 78th Special Operations Unit as a Russian Voice Intercept Operator and Transcriber. That was in 1963-64, while I was an enlisted man (See Chapter 5). The second was that my file continued after my service at USMLM. There are entries about my tour of teaching at USMA and my serving as an Assistant Army Attaché in Moscow, which was in 1979-81. Further, there is an entry about my being promoted to lieutenant colonel in 1982, after I had returned to the U.S. from my Moscow assignment.

Some of the pages in these materials were in Russian, but they too contained more or less the same information that was on the German pages. My physical description in Russian was the same. One wonders whether a Soviet or an East German observer submitted the original report. The somewhat comical physical description leads to a more important question: How skewed or incorrect were operational reports on me and other Allied Mission members?

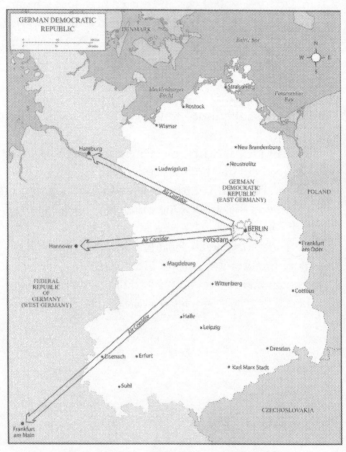

Map 1: German Democratic Republic

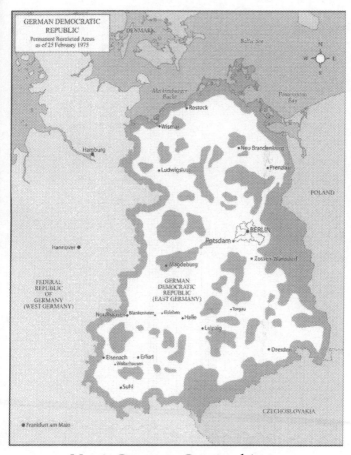

Map 2: Permanent Restricted Areas

Sources

Aldrich, Richard J. *the hidden hand.* The Overlook Press, Woodstock and New York, 2001.

Cooper, Don. *A Trick.* Pale Bone Publishing, San Diego, 2000.

Craven, John Piña. *The Silent War.* A Touchstone Book. Simon & Schuster, New York, 2001.

Dulles, Allen. *The Craft of Intelligence.* Harper and Row, Publishers, Inc. New York, 1963.

_____. *Great True Spy Stories.* [Unidentified Chinese publisher, 1968]

Fahey, John. *Licensed to Spy.* Naval Institute Press. Annapolis, 2002.

Geraghty, Tony. *BRIXMIS.* HarperCollins, London, 1997.

Gibson, Steve. *The Last Mission Behind the Iron Curtain.* Sutton Publishing Limited. Phoenix Mill, Thrupp, Stroud, Gloucestershire, Great Britain, 1997.

Herrington, Stuart A. *Traitors Among Us.* A Harvest Book, Harcourt, Inc. San Diego, New York, London, 1999.

Lewis, William J. *The Warsaw Pact: Arms, Doctrine, and Strategy.* McGraw-Hill Publications Co. New York, 1982.

Murphy, David E., Sergei A. Kondrashev and George Bailey, *Battleground Berlin.* Yale University Press. New Haven and London, 1997.

Seman, Timothy A. Cold War Intelligence: United States Military Liaison Mission, 1947-1990. Unpublished M.A. Thesis, The American University, U.S. DC, 1994.

Skowronek, Paul, U.S. Soviet Military Liaison in Germany Since 1947. Unpublished PhD dissertation, University of Colorado, 1976.

Stafford, David. *Spies Beneath Berlin.* The Overlook Press. Woodstock and New York, 2002.

Story of BRIXMIS 1946-1990, The. The BRIXMIS Association, 1993. (No publisher location given.)

Trastour, Daniel. *La guerre sans armes.* Éditions des Écrivains, Paris, 2001.

USMLM Unit Histories, 1964-1969, 1971-79, 1981-86, 1988. Available at www.history.hqusareur.army.mil/uslmannual.htm.

Index

T

About the Author

James Holbrook began his U.S. Army career as a private and retired as a lieutenant colonel. He served with the U.S. Military Liaison Mission in Potsdam, East Germany and West Berlin in 1976-1977.

Before the Mission assignment, Holbrook worked at all levels of intelligence—as an enlisted Russian linguist in West Berlin, commanding officer of an intelligence detachment in South Vietnam, and as an operational and strategic analyst in the Pentagon and Europe. He was awarded the Legion of Merit, two Bronze Stars, the Meritorious Service Medal, the Army Commendation Medal and several service and campaign ribbons.

The author holds BA and MA degrees from The American University and a PhD from Georgetown.